Standing On His Words

By: Simené Walden

Standing On His Words: Prayers and Devotionals Every Educator Can Pray

Published by The Student Teacher in association with Ingram Spark.

Co-Editors: Belinda Rainwater and Simene' Walden

Cover: Jamil Abbas

ISBN: 978-0-9997987-1-3

Scriptures are taken from the King James Bible and New Living Translation unless otherwise noted.

About the Author

R.J.H Photography

Simené Walden, also known as "The Student Teacher", was given that name by the Holy Ghost on June 7, 2016, during an early morning chat session. She is a teacher by vocation, but is always in a place of learning something new that will catapult her to the next level in her destiny. Simené worked as a middle school Language Arts teacher in the state of North Carolina for twelve years, and now teaches in the state of Maryland.

Simené was born in Hertford County, North Carolina, and was raised in Northampton County, North Carolina. She attended Northampton County Public Schools, and upon graduating she went to Fayetteville State University. In the process of a five-year span, she attended three different colleges only to find herself back where she started, namely, Fayetteville State University. In 2004, Simené graduated from Fayetteville State University with a Bachelor of Arts degree in English & Literature. Ten years later, she graduated from Grand Canyon University with a Master's of Arts degree in Christian Studies with an emphasis on Youth Ministry.

Simene' believes in being teachable and always in a posture of learning even from those one may not think has anything to offer. Everyone has something to offer. Her primary objective is to teach others everything she has learned so they, too, can be empowered, educated, and equipped. "The Student Teacher's" goal through this book is to encourage and empower individuals to pray and believe God for the miraculous within the educational gates. If God is not glorified, it becomes vain and an idol. God is a jealous God and any other gods that we put before Him will die by fire, in the name of Jesus.

Simene' is active in her local church, Temple of Praise International Church, in Beltsville, Maryland, where she serves in various ministries. You can find her serving and sharing Jesus on the streets of DC regularly as well as on her social media. Simené has a heart for the youth and has a desire to see radical changes among them. She has recently launched her academic consulting business, *The Student Teacher.*

Contact the author:

thestudentteacher17@gmail.com

http://www.simenewalden.com

https://www.facebook.com/thestudenteacher

http://www.twitter.com/@simenewalden

http://periscope.tv/@simenewalden

http://instagram.com/simenewalden

Mailing Address: PO Box 813 Savage, MD 20763

Be sure to sign up for The Student Teacher's newsletter on the website to always receive the latest news, offers, and events from Author Simene' Walden.

For Course Offerings, Workshops, Programs, Booking Inquiries and Speaking Engagements, please contact the author via email or follow the link on her website.

Dedication

This book is dedicated to the many people who helped shape me into the person I am today and the educator I strive to be. Thank you, to all the women who have poured into me, helped pull me out of a life of perversion, and continue to help me in the various areas of my life. Without your guidance, mentoring, and love, I would have never stepped into marketplace ministry.

I could never say enough about the woman who birthed me and raised me. My mother continues to nurture me in new ways. Mom, I dedicate this book to you because you loved me endlessly when I was an endlessly unlovable person. Without your support and love, I am not sure if I would even be here today. You are the best mother in the world and the absolute best mother for me.

To my Aunt Sandra, who has supported me from the beginning of this journey, I appreciate and love you so much.

To every child and every student whom I have ever had the privilege of teaching or interacting with – thank you. This book is because of you and for you. You are the generation where no child will be left behind. These prayers will carry you to your next dimension in God. God will raise up godly men and women to teach and impart in you like never before.

My Lord and Savior, You are not the last Person I recognize to dedicate this book to, rather I have dedicated my life to You. This book is only one of the ways I want to say thank You publicly for life and life more abundantly. Holy Spirit, You gave me the words to say. Lord Jesus, You gave me breath in my body and the ability to articulate and write out what You spoke to me. I owe You my life. This is Your book and I give it back to You. I love you Father!

Contents

Acknowledgements

Ishall take my time to thank all of you who have played a major role in my life because my success, deliverance, and healing has manifested from being divinely connected to all of you. To those of you whom I did not specifically mention, know that I am grateful for you, too, but some names I could not remember, but I see your faces and remember your love.

In my opinion, I have had some of the best instructors, teachers, and assistants that have ever lived. However, there is only one **Teresa Warren** and only one **Eunice Reid**. Mrs. Warren was my first and second grade teacher at Willis Hare Elementary School. She is a petite white lady who never raised her voice and always gave us manila folders to put on our desks whenever we took our weekly test. I so loved that lady and I still have so much love for her. Thank you for connecting with me on social media and I remember you sending me a card and gift when I graduated college. I cherish that moment and will forever keep the card. It was as if I was a second grader all over again.

Northampton County Schools, I love you. August 2015, I left prayers for the school system in the door of the central office. Whether they were distributed to the staff or not,

God heard them as I prayed and He shall turn that district around for His glory.

Thank you, **Willis Elementary School.** Thank you, Mrs. Patricia Earquhart, Mrs. Veronica Daye, Ms. Susie Goode, and the late Mrs. Ethel Hawkins. Thank you, to all of my elementary school friends.

Thank you, **Conway Middle School.** Thank you, Ms. Trigg Branch, Ms. Rosa Vaughan, Mr. Jethro Branch, Mrs. Helen Wilkins, Mrs. Daughtry, Mrs. Rhonda Moses, and Ms. Lisa Wheeler. Thank you, to every other staff member who provided me with a safe and orderly environment to learn in every day.

Thank you, **Northampton County High School-East.** Thank you, to all the teachers and the ones who made a huge difference in my life. I would like to give a special thank you to Mrs. Vivian Hunter, Mr. Mark Curry, Mr. DeSilva, Mr. Harris, aka, "Cat Daddy", Mrs. Natasha Brown Stephenson, Mr. Brock Womble, Mrs. Josephine Dunn, Mr. Charles Tyner, Mrs. Ronnie Pfeiffer, Ms. Gordon, Mrs. Felicia Wyche-Whitaker, Ms. Walters, and Ms. Heather Seanor.

Thank you, to all of my high school friends *and* foes. You have encouraged me to be all that God intended for me.

Thank you, **Northampton County Board of Education Staff**, who allowed me to work with them even as an assistant to the superintendent my last year in high school. Thank you, James Pickens, Natalie Grant, and Patricia Harris.

Thank you, **Upward Bound Program**. I am thankful for every instructor, counselor, and person I met. One of my best friends and I had some good times at Chowan College. I love and miss you **Kimberly Shearin**. Save my place in heaven. I will be there in another hundred years.

Thank you, **Douglas Byrd Middle School** staff for welcoming me with open arms my first year of teaching. I had no idea what to do but I had the amazing Ms. Audrey Pipkins-Suggs, Ms. Erica Sullivan, Mr. William Wesley, Ms. Justine Jones, Mrs. Inette Smith-Brothers, Ms. Erica Jones, Ms. Lisa Henderson, Ms. Sonia Cameron, Mrs. Stephanie Carver, Ms. Katie Cosby, Ms. Sacola Lehr, Ms. Valerie Martin, Ms. Amanda Suggs, Ms. Christine Abbey, Mrs. Daisha Colvin, Ms. Linda Gray, and Ms. Michelle Dillon.

Thank you, to my seventh-grade team and all of the students I have had the privilege to teach. Thank you Kayla Fairley, Amber Brookins, Jessica Blue, Dennis Vasquez, Tyreka McKinnon, Tyrek Alston, Ariel Avant, Galina Azeeva, Briana Baker, Yamilexa Benitaz, Thaddeus Barbee,

Elizabeth Black, Kristin Braxton, Dezaree Brooks, Tonya Bingham, Calatha Butler, Shauntavia Burrell-Fallon, Rachel Ramos, Alexis Sanchez, Luis Carmona, Derrius Carson, Jamison Caulder, Natalie Cole, Michael Coleman, Jaqueline Dezaren, Carlotte Drake, Tiffany Edwards, Jamie Fields, Ashley Finch, Tiffany Fowler, Phillip Frazier, Paige Gilbert, Jeremiah Gann, Nonde Gordon, Tifanni Gregory, Naomi Hardy, Nicholas Hargrave, Detavius Harper, Stephanie Hartman, Kayla Henderson, Airreon Hoking,

Nantecia Jackson, Aaron Jones, Shonequa Keels, Malissa Lewis, Mykela Lilly, Tanisha Love, Cory Magnum, Bonnie Martinez, Derek McLaurin, Torri Montgomery, Phillip Murphy, Yung-Hsiang Yeh, Gabriela Paulino, Christina Ratley, Sequioa Heyward, Lisa Waananen, Destiny Woodard, Felicia Underwood, Rai'Chell Turner, Shelby Thompson, Erin Starnes, Eric Sims, Jessica Slade, Nicholas Sessions, Kenneth Short, Kayla Salter- Williams, Shanquella Ross, Brandon Reeves, Darryl Robinson, Isaiah Robinson, and the late Gabriel Waters.

Pamela Cromartie, hands down you have been the best assistant principal I have ever worked with. You were professional, fair, godly, stern, and pleasant to be around. I know I let you down when I never took the opportunity to work with you again, and didn't even call you back to say I changed my mind, but you have always been in my heart.

Back then, I was too afraid to confront issues or say no. So, excuse the immature Ms. Walden. Please welcome and receive the mature, confident Ms. Walden.

Erika Jones, may this book find you and let you know how much of a help you were to me my first year of teaching. You helped me get through the worst day of my teaching career, to date. Of course, we both probably remember it like it was yesterday when our sweet student, Gabriel, went home to be with the Lord. If you had not been on my team, I do not think I could have gotten through that year. Thank you, for always being supportive and loving. I love you and I hope to reunite with you again.

Thank you, *Jackson Middle School* staff. Thank you, Mr. Jason Johnson, Ms. Rita Tisdale, Ms. Saletta Urenas, Mrs. Danielle Gabrielle, Mr. Carmen Farlow, Ms. Sue McLawhorn, Mrs. Karen Braswell, and Ms. Nealy.

Thank you, to all the eighth-grade students I taught, and the eighth-grade staff. I would like to give a special thank you to Juquasia Robinson, Justin "Teddy" Clark, David Amerson, Marie Be, Jessica Douangprachanh Chen, Andrea Ingram, Angelica Shaw, and Adrian "Scooter".

Thank you, *Elliotte Nelson*. God placed you on my heart to reach out and look for you on Facebook. I am forever blessed to have contacted you, apologized to you for the way I treated you as my student, and your willingness to forgive me. The love of God poured from my heart on that October 1, 2015 night, and I was forever changed.

Guilford Preparatory Academy, you guys rock. You truly were my family. Vatricia "Officer" Jenkins-Void, Mrs. Maria Ardila, Mrs. Rehana Sultana, Ms. Helen Johnson, Mrs. Umesh, Mrs. Kimberly Douglas, Ms. Sheresha Russell, Mr. Duncan Butler, Ms. Valerie McClain, the late Mrs. Twann Burke, you all made my career there worthwhile. Love you all.

Thank you, to the entire middle school staff and the middle school students. Thank you, Whitney Parks, LaPrecious Carter, Justice Wall, Tobi Saliu, Alicia Scoggins, Michael Bass, Tyrone Woodard, Michael Heber, Shaddiah Crandell, Akiya Daye, Merghani Elboshra, Michael Heber, Jolie Gallitelli, Mrs. Jamallah Harris, Jordan Collins, and the countless other students that I taught and loved. You all made me want to be better.

Thank you, *Vatricia Jenkins-Void*. It was pretty awkward working at GPA for the first few weeks, but I got acclimated fast. Thank you, for always making work feel like play. You were good and saved back then, while I was good and sinning. Thanks for the praise breaks every morning. It started my day off just right. Thanks for inviting me to your church and loving me even when I was living a life totally opposite to yours. Thanks for bringing me along with your husband after work. We had some really good times before and after work. You are a great teacher, good friend, and a great coach.

Thank you, **Mrs. Robin Buckrham**. There is so much I can say about you, but the two words that I can never say enough are, 'Thank you'. You gave me a chance when I had just gotten fired from my position with the county. You believed in me when I did not believe in myself. You pushed me and groomed me into a great language arts teacher. You coached me along the way and saw me mature right before your eyes. Of course, I cannot forget those moments when we wanted to do damage to one another, but through the good, bad, and ugly, you were a great principal to work for. More importantly, you have continued to be a great mentor after I was no longer an employee under your direct supervision.

Thank you, **Northridge Middle School** staff. Thank you, Ms. Barrino, Mr.Crawford, Mr. Barnes, Ms. Cassandra Gates, Mrs. Shantell McKinney, Ms.Makeda Holley, Ms. Lisa Clark, Mr. Benjamin Cabeza, Mr. Jones, Mr. Darrell Peterson, Ms. Tiffany Washington, Tyler Bolden, Iris McConneyhead, Melissa Mingo, Bridgett Wiley, Willie Barley, Crasharnia Harman, Billy Hopkins, Clifton Jones, Mrs. Kyle Polk, Ms.

Crystal Kelly, Ms. Rachel Lewis, Ms. Evelyn Massey, Ms. Karla Naughton, Ms. Marie Pacini, Ms. Valerie Ruff, Ms. Jacci Tyes, Ms. Lequana Able, Ms. Delisha Covington, Ms. Chasity Cussac, Ms. Laquisha Miller, and Ms. Rebecca George.

Thank you, to my seventh-grade team and students. Thank you, Christopher Baldwin, Kayla Barrett, Leyah Barringer, Rashad Brannon, Narya Brown, Caelei Brown, Kane Browning, Chase Bruton, Shaheim Cannie, Miyana Dunlap, Makayla Carter, Jordan Coggins, Shahquan Cureton, Ray Cruz, Daniel Delancy, Kevin Eguizabal, Stefany Esparza, Christopher Funderburk, Luis Gomez Merino, Jadah Greene, Aujalaeyah Hamilton-Burto, Destine Harrington, Shari Harris, Adnane Hedadja, Megan Hernandez, Johnathan Hobson, Christian Hoey, Jaylen Holley, Mariane Hout, Cameron Jackson, Tia Johnson, Khalid Lamont, Matthew Lopez, Joseph Hugo, Jacari Major, Edwin Martinez, Anastasie Mbaya, Jose Meija, Kayla Pastures, Rafael Perez, Kelsea Ratchford, Jazmine Rouser, Xykeira Sims, Rashaad Sinclair, Kailyn Smith, Romeo Stephens, Crystal Vazquez, Raul Villa, Amir Walker, Rachel Walker, Kenneth White, Demonica Wright, Kesahn Artis, Kaela Wright, and Kenari Wright.

Thank you, *Enfield Middle School* staff and students. Thank you, Ms. Jacqueline Williams, Mr. Robert Hunter,

Mrs. Carolyn Mitchell, Ms. Nekkiia McGee, Ms. Shiquitta Mason. Thank you, Joquez Davis, Alphonso Rudd, and Spier Whitaker.

Thank you, **Ms. Jacqueline Williams**. I knew there was something uniquely different about you when I spoke to you over the phone. Your soft mannerism and your professionalism made me work extremely hard under your leadership. The one year working with you was the toughest year personally for me as a teacher, and I know God placed you in my path for no other reason than that. I do not know how I would have survived dealing with an aunt dying of cancer and my good friend at the same time, without your unwavering support. You never questioned the days I needed to be off, and you never gave me a hard time. I truly appreciate you and I can't wait to see all the doors God will open for you. You're an awesome administrator.

Thank you, **Alphonso Rudd**. You taught me what it meant to love your job and not do it for benefits or income. You would always say I was preaching. Now, I really am. I love you. Thank you for pushing me into my purpose and making me a better person. I am forever grateful you crossed my path.

Thank you, **Marquasha Brinkley**. You were one tough cookie, but I love you so much. You are a very intelligent young woman, whom I want to see do nothing but excel in life and enjoy the fruits of your labor. Allow God to direct your steps and you will be blown away by how He blesses your life.

Thank you, **Sugar Creek Charter School** staff. Ms. Shiquitta Mason, Ms. Kimberly Byrd, Ms. Iva Bishop, Mrs. Renee Miller-Nahgahwon, Mr. Jamal Young, Ms. Celeste Sundo, Ms.Charlotte Anderson, Mrs. Keisha Hillocks, Mr. Josef Walls, Mr. Lathan Black, Mr. Andy Samuel, Mr. Patrick Torrence, Mr. Kevin Megan, Mr. Javies, Mrs. Carina Richmond Livingston, Ms. Xavier Johnson, Ms. Tawana Wiggins, Mrs. Alisha Harris, Mr. Marlon Harris, Ms. Evertte, Mr. Jarod Bridges, Mr. Jerome Lyles, Mr. Marquis Mason, Mr. Tory Jones, Mrs. Markita Withers McGowan, Mrs. Janette Brown, and Mrs. Mechelle.

Thank you, **Kimberly Byrd**, for your friendship. I learned many, many things from you. Your leadership and love for the children inspired me. You pushed me to be the best me. You encouraged me when I wanted to quit and give up. You spoke life into me when I was fearful and scared. You spoke many of the things I am currently doing in the educational arena into existence. You wrote papers for school, highlighting what I was doing and where God was taking me.

They all shall come to pass by the grace of God and for His glory. I love you and Bryce Byrd.

Thank you, **Shiquitta Mason,** for all of your support. Even when you had to stand alone to support me, thank you. I thank God for connecting me with you in Halifax County for my divine connection to Sugar Creek. You are the only person I have ever worked with at two different schools that was in two totally different counties. God strategically placed us together. You have been rocking with this Educational Prayer Network from its inception and I appreciate your love and support. May the kingdom of God be your portion. May these prayers change the atmosphere and dynamics of the students you teach in Ahu Dhabi. God answered our very prayer for this as we started to petition God on the prayer call. He amazes me every day.

Thank you, **Iva Bishop.** You have always been so supportive and encouraging. Thank you for always standing and believing in me. Thank you for giving me wise counsel and good advice. Thank you for being an example of a hard and diligent worker, and a great educator.

Thank you, **Ms. Cheryl Turner,** for giving me an opportunity to work at Sugar Creek and lead at Sugar Creek. Thank you for trusting me to step out and take the students on an out-of-state field trip. What the devil meant for evil, God surely turned it for His good. God bless you for the work you have done at Sugar Charter School and the legacy you will leave.

Thank you, **Dominia Blount**, for your leadership and your genuine love and support. You supported the girls' group and you even sat in on a session that was held at Sugar Creek. You are a very intelligent woman and I so look forward to all God has in store for you and your children.

Thank you, **Celeste Sundo**. Thank you for always taking my calls when I called out. Smile. But thank you for being easy to talk to and supportive while I was at Sugar Creek.

Thank you, **Renee Nahgahgwon**. You opened my eyes to many things, including my flaws. I became a better person for listening to your advice.

Thank you, **Mother's and Daughter's Mentoring Group**. Thank you for allowing me to be a part of and share what God had given me to do at such a time as that. Thank you, Ms. Sylvia Allen, Mrs. Perneice, and Jah' Nichols' mom.

Thank you, **University City Church**, for allowing members to create small groups that would impact the community. Thank you *Pastor Michael and Sharon Stevens* for your leadership. Thank you to *Andrea Hodge* for your mentorship and wise counsel.

Thank you to the small group, *TRIAD*, which was the vision of one very brilliant woman. Thank you, *Ms. Rochelle Gray* for your vision, leadership, and love for children. Thank you, *Mrs. Cheryl Monosanto* and *Ms. Jesse Campbell*, for working diligently with TRIAD. Thank you for trusting that I would be a good host, and I truly hope I was.

I give many thanks to my special mentor the late *Dawn Marie Mayfield* and her husband *Mr. Wendell Mayfield*.

Thank you, *Buck Lodge Middle School* staff and students. Thank you to all of my former and current students.

Thank you, *Mr. Kenneth Nance.* Thank you so much for your leadership. The work you do at Buck Lodge does not go unnoticed. I pray many blessings upon you and may the Lord call you to duplicate what you have done and will do at Buck Lodge across the DMV area. May you open your own school in the way students are educated.

Thank you, *Ms. Marie Leonard.* You are a great administrator and you have a very warm spirit. Thank you for being able to agree to disagree with me in a respectful way. We will look back over it all four years from now and have a different conversation. Thank you so much for all of your support, help, and work in the classroom, especially with the students who have disabilities.

Thank you, **Mrs. Aja Ramsay**. God told me a few months after I started working at Buck Lodge that he would show me favor on my job and it would come by way of Rich Square. I had no idea what that meant, but now I know. I appreciate the push you give me and the practical, helpful advice and critique. May every door you desire to be open never be closed, in Jesus' name.

Thank you, to **every educator** who has taught me, whether it was in the area of academics, ministry, or personal needs and growth. Over a period of thirteen years, I have taught so many wonderful students. Some have stuck with me through the years and social media has allowed us to keep in touch, while others I have not spoken to or seen, but you all have a special place in my heart.

Thank you, to all of my **former and current administrators, colleagues, and supervisors**. I appreciate your leadership. Thank you to every administrator who ever interviewed me and either offered me the job or went with another applicant.

Thank you, Ms. Lodies Gloston, Mrs. Pamela Cromartie, Mr. Mike Coram, Mr. Jason Johnson, Ms. Rachel Lewis, Ms. Kimberly Hazel, Mr. Crawford, Mrs. Robin Buckrham, Mr.

Lewis Baker, Ms. Jacqueline Williams, Ms. Cheryl Turner, Ms. Dominia Blount, Mr. James Richardson, Mr. Kenneth Nance, Ms. Marie Leonard, Mrs. Aja Ramsay, Ms. Duran, and Mr. Richard Belton. Thank you to every superintendent and school board. Thank you to every politician and governmental employee who supports and works in the educational system.

Thank you, to all of my *current and former students*, you have pushed me to be a better person.

Thank you, to my current **Buck Lodge Middle School students**. I love you all so much. You have been the most respectful, loving students I have had in my twelve years of teaching. I look forward to coming to school every day to see you guys. Pursue your dreams and do not allow stereotypes, disabilities, dilemmas, or the negative thoughts and opinions of others keep you from obtaining all you desire. You all are very intelligent and you will change this world around. Your kind words and sincere hearts have helped me through my illness. This book is for you and your children's children. I love you guys. To all the "Cheese Touch" kids, you will forever have the cheese touch.

Thank you, to my best friend, ***Cierra Patrice Thompson-White***, I love you. You have been the best support I could ask for throughout my career as a teacher. You shared many ideas with me on classroom management, lesson planning, and lots of funny stories. More students, besides the ones I teach, need to see your plays. It is your time, boo.

To my spiritual mother, **Evangelist Rita Bowman**, thank you. Thank you for being in place at the right time to receive me. With loving kindness and tenderness, you nursed me back to life. You gave spiritual birth to me after you carried me for months. I will never forget that conversation. Your firm, sound, biblical knowledge, advice, and teachings have brought me to a place I could only imagine. The pureness of your heart and the love you have for God and His people is one-of-a-kind. I am forever grateful to you because you lovingly demanded that I have an authentic relationship with God. Your prayers and fiery teachings broke me out of bondage. I do not think I could have ever written this book without first meeting you and becoming equipped for what was ahead. Thank you so much. I love you.

To my pastor, prophet, and apostle, **Nike Wilheims**, God bless you. You pour out effortlessly and relentlessly. From the moment I connected with you, my life has been better. Your wisdom, counsel, and love have pushed me through some of my toughest moments. Emotionally, I was a wreck when the Lord sent me to your church, but the prayers that have been prayed over me, literally rerouted my destiny.

When I wanted to backslide on God, you prayed me through and provided sound counsel and wisdom. My prayer life has soared since being a member of Temple of Praise International Church. It was you who prayed over me and released the prayer mantle of Jehu in my life. I've never been the same. I now know how to pray scripture and I do not know how I ever prayed without it.

Thank you to all the listeners that have participated and will participate in the Educational Prayer Call and Network. We are going to shift some things by the finger of God.

I AM NOT WHAT I AM ON MY OWN!

Empowering Educators Through Prayer

Facebook Post from May 20, 2016

God will back his Word if you have faith enough to believe it. A mighty wind, the East Wind, the wind that parted the Red Sea, the Euroclydon Wind is blowing out all of the wickedness in the educational system. We have to stand on what we believe and fight. Time out for being passive and lukewarm. The fight you had in the world is the fight times 1000 you need as a Christ follower. The fight you have for other people, needs to be diverted to the enemy and his wicked plans. Jesus has come to the schools and your children will be protected because he has set his angels over those buildings. Who can stand and fight against the Lord without being utterly destroyed?

"And the kings of the earth, and the great men, and the rich men, and the chief captains, and the mighty men, and every bondman, and every free man, hid themselves in the dens and in the rocks of the mountains; And said to the mountains and rocks, Fall on us, and hide us from the face of him that sitteth on the throne, and from the wrath of the Lamb: For the great day of his wrath is come; and who shall be able to stand?" (Rev. 6:15-17 King James Version)

Empowering Educators Through Prayer is for everyone. If you are not a parent then you are at least someone's child, whether they are living or deceased. We all came from the womb of a woman. With that being said, we are all called to be educators in some aspect in our lives. We may be educators in our homes with our families, educators in our careers, educators while running our businesses, educators within our religious organizations, educators within our community, political arenas, music, media, or fashion industry. We may be educators in the educational system, whether it is public or private. We may be educators while being educated in a school, course, class, college, or university. Men and women both are educators in their own respective ways with their own way of approaching things.

This network of educators encompasses individuals from all socioeconomic backgrounds, social statuses, religions, races, educational backgrounds, and career and job occupations.

This network reflects the diversity of this nation and the world in which we live. I would be remiss to think that this is the only group of individuals praying for the school system, because it is not. There are many well organized, long-standing organizations that have been interceding on my behalf as an educator, as well as you and your children for decades. But, this is the only group of individuals God has called me to pray with and gather with. The educational system has been under attack for many years, but now people are really taking notice. With the increase of violence in schools, sexual laws being forced upon our children, courses and classes that contradict many peoples' personal beliefs that are required by many states for elementary students–something drastic has to be done. Prayer isn't a drastic measure because it should have never been taken out of the school, but now we have to create a circuit in the spirit, unite for all children everywhere, and petition God to heal our land and keep our babies safe and protected.

I've heard many parents say they would die for their kids. I get the extremity and passion you have for your child or children, but in reality, if you die for them and they live, who becomes responsible for them? Who will raise and rear them? Who will innately have a passion and a love for them like you? Our words shape our world. Be careful what comes out your mouth. Don't die for your child. Live for you child. Intercede for your child. Stand on the wall for your child. Be a godly example for your child.

Parents, you are the first teachers your child will know. Think about when you are teaching them to walk, to use the potty, to ride a bike, to count, to say their abc's, and to say mama and dada. Those moments of success excite you, and they should. As an educator for over eleven years, I find joy in seeing children succeed and accomplish goals, large or small. My focus on education has shifted a bit and now I focus more on educating the whole child, which starts with character. Children attend school with a plethora of issues every day and we expect them to sit down quietly in a traditional classroom and be a model student. That does not happen very often and as the world turns, I think we are going to see that less and less.

Children carry parental problems in their heart. They battle with depression, suicide, cutting, low self-esteem, and body image issues. Many have been sexually assaulted and violated, beat down with words and labels, and when they dibble and dabble in sex, drugs, alcohol, pornography (the internet has it all), lying, cheating, stealing, raping, killing, and the like, then we take notice. Black crime, and crime for that matter, has been an issue for decades. The same children who didn't listen years ago to their own parents are now parents of the children committing many of these crimes today. Instead of chastising their children, they condoned it, laughed at it, paraded them around to perform for others, all while perpetuating a cycle of rebellion and disrespect for authority.

So, the uphill fight is not to just cover and pray for the children and our schools, but to cover and pray for the families that send these children to school. The Bible commands us to honor our mothers and fathers. This was not a conditional statement. It doesn't matter what they have done or what they will do, we are to honor them and watch how God allows our own children to honor us. We have to pray for the educators who are standing before our children and the law makers who implement policies that affect our children and the educational system. Please do not ever say you do not have anything to pray for. Our honest answer is we don't have a burden or we haven't set aside time to pray. Let's all do our part. One person praying could chase 1,000 demons away. Two people praying, especially about the same thing or the same situation can chase 10,000 demons away. Your words are powerful. Use them, and watch God.

Introduction

This book of prayers and devotionals was birthed out of my struggle, burden, and desire to see the children I taught and currently teach healed in every area of their lives. I used to be like the teachers and educators that I pray for in this book. I am still growing in many areas, but the Lord has brought me a long way and I am not who I was when I began my teaching career. I believe God has a desire to shift the educational system to include his Word, and daily prayer recitation. God gave me a vision of what the schools–the public schools–will look like if we all start praying His will in heaven to be done on this earth. I believe it was on January 5, 2017 when God gave me a vision of what these prayers can accomplish.

God showed me a day would come when kids would be walking outside for physical education, praying and pleading the blood of Jesus over their buildings. Students would start prayer groups, praying at the bus stops, praying at games, praying at practice, praying in the locker rooms, praying for their peers at dances, at proms, on senior trips. I see students praying in the cafeteria, in the hallways, during dismissal from and arrival to school. I see prayer cell groups suddenly bursting out in the schools, universities, colleges, community and technical colleges, in the teachers' lounges, in the parking lots, on the buses, in Jesus name.

I have seen a day when kids would be speaking in tongues in your classroom, laying hands on the sick and they recover. Nurses will be in place for protocol, law, and precautions, but the chief physician will show up on the scene. I see it. I see it. I saw it. I saw it. I see a day when kids who are not believers will ask their other believing classmates to pray for them, lay hands on them, and pray for their families because they will see the demonstration of God and the tangible manifestations of answered prayers in their lives. God showed that to me in the spirit. I am pretty sure I was not daydreaming that.

I can see headlines now, 'Students Get Suspended for Disrupting School With Prayer'. They will sell it as it was a distraction but it will have shifted so many things in the system that they will have to put kingdom kids out to re-strategize.

While they are waiting to go home, they will gather and pray in the offices. Their suspension will be a time for God to download even more insight and revelation into them. God has given them the ears of the learned so even when they do not have perfect attendance in school, they will have perfect attendance in the kingdom. They will not miss work and they will not be left behind. In fact, they will excel, be at the top of their class, and be farther ahead of their peers when they return. Who can stand and fight against the Lord without being utterly destroyed?

"And the kings of the earth, and the great men, and the rich men, and the chief captains, and the mighty men, and every bondman, and every free man, hid themselves in the dens and in the rocks of the mountains; And said to the mountains and rocks, Fall on us, and hide us from the face of Him that sitteth on the throne, and from the wrath of the Lamb: For the great day of His wrath is come; and who shall be able to stand?"(Rev. 6:15-17 King James Version)

A day will come on the prayer call on Sunday nights when I will not be leading it, but it will be led by students who will be old, young, and middle aged. There will be a day that I will not be the only one leading school prayers, but people from across this nation will be praying and scoping it. I see it and it is impossible for me to do it all, and I do not want to do it all. I am assured that is why God has given me the Empowering Educators Through Prayer Network.

While the enemies are re-strategizing, the kingdom of God still is and will be advancing. And everything we shall do will be done in decency and order. I pray this book blesses you, your children, and your children's children.

Standing on His Word, Volume 1: Teacher's Edition is a 31-Day Prayer Devotional. These prayers and devotions have been birthed in the secret place of God. God would daily give me fresh downloads from heaven.

Had God not sent me to a wilderness place in the state of Maryland, I would not have known what I had on the inside. Do not curse your wilderness place or your wilderness experience. I didn't understand that until I read Revelation 12:6. God had prepared the wilderness for the woman.

My wilderness place was, too, prepared by God and I was to take up residence there for some time. Sometimes he has to get you by yourself to speak to you, deal with you, rebuke you, chasten you, love you, clean you, and then prepare you. Never curse your wilderness experience.

My pastor, Apostle Nike Wilheims, gave me a prayer mantle on Sunday, November 27, 2016, and she prayed over me at the end of service. She prayed that a spirit of prayer would come upon me. She prayed that I would be a fisher of men. She prayed that the mantle of Daniel, the mantle of Jehu, and a double mantle of prayer be released upon me. Since then, my prayer life has gone to another level. Find someone who can speak life into you. You will know an apostle because they will reduplicate themselves by way of the people they shepherd, pour into, and send out. The Holy Ghost has released me. We are here now.

Our goal, our return on investment is souls for the kingdom and the only way to overturn the things that have happened is through prayer. Once we pray and God gives us instructions, we execute with wisdom, knowledge, and understanding.

"For God chose to save us through our Christ, not to pour out his anger on us. Christ died for us so that, whether we are dead or alive when he returns, we can live with him forever. So encourage each other and build each other up, just as you are already Lord Jesus doing". (1 Thess. 5:9-11 New Living Translation)

For those of you that are not even saved, God wants to save your soul more so than be upset with you. We serve a good, good God. He does get upset, in fact, the Word says in Psalms 7:11 that God is angry with the wicked all day, but He desires to receive you in His kingdom.

When God led me to a verse of Scripture in Isaiah, my tenacity and zeal to pen these words and get these books into the hands of millions of readers went to another level.

"Now go and write down these words. Write them in a book. They will stand until the end of time as a witness that these people are stubborn rebels who refuse to pay attention to the LORD's instructions." (Isa. 30:8-9 New Living Translation)

Who Are the Educators Educating Your Child?

D o not waste your time trying to correct those who have purposed in their hearts that they will reject what you say. Correct those who are wise and who want to be taught. Someone's disrespect should not negate your desire for and manifestation of respect.

Carnal people will never understand spiritual things. As long as God is fighting for you, you're good. You know how they did Jesus, right? One minute he was the greatest and then some of those same people turned around and crucified him. I have an intercessor who is praying for me. When you tell people, God is fighting for you, it sounds funny because they use people to fight for them. Now that's a laugh in itself. Man is no match for the one and only true living God.

Education is not like a factory or production plant. If there is a defective product produced, you can discard it and get another one. You can even send it back and get a replacement. As an educator, we do not have the luxury of producing poorly educated individuals and if they are not effective, we can discard them and get another one. We may lock them up, ignore them, or kill them, but it does not stop the problem of a mass distribution of defective students. Parents, be informed. Some people sitting in front of your child are not fit. And they don't have to be a sex offender or lacking a degree to be considered "not fit". Do surprise visits to the schools not to check up on your child, but to check up on us. Make sure we're doing right by your child. And when you come, make sure you're doing right by your child, too. It's a partnership between us. We have to bridge the gap between parents, teachers, and students.

As an educator, I see children robbed of opportunities every day because adults don't want to do something or don't feel like doing something. I see children robbed of opportunities every day because teachers want to stick to the same thing they have been doing since the beginning of their educational career, or too lazy or too sick to learn and do something else. Children are robbed of opportunities because some educators are intimidated by something else due to past experiences, or just too stubborn to do the "new" that is required or expected. Many students are robbed of opportunities because educators are overworked, overwhelmed, and burned out. Unfortunately, many will not retire or find another job because they are too comfortable in the one they have, they simply need the benefits, or they know they are not competent enough to do another job at the level required. Many people hide behind tenure, longevity, or unions, when in actuality, they are doing more harm than good by staying. When we're in the customer service business, sometimes we have to do things that stretch us beyond our comfort zones. Many people know what to say at the right time, but few follow through during the toughest times. I know and see the politics and policies that are in place that tie one hand behind our backs on many levels, but what are we doing to be fair and impactful to all children with the one free hand we have?

I wonder what is the rate at which children have been labeled because it challenges or challenged the teaching style and personality of the one educating them?

I wonder how many children have been incorrectly placed on a certain track or in a certain class based solely on the personality and preface of the one who may have already educated them or the one who will educate them?

I wonder how many children aren't even exposed to material that challenges them but has it watered down because of the assumptions made about them?

I wonder how many children are cursed to their faces (not necessarily with curse words) on a regular basis from the adult standing in front of them?

I wonder how many educators are really burned out from teaching, but are too afraid or intimidated to do something else? Many educators don't even have the capacity to teach this generation of children so they hide behind tenure or longevity in their schools.

I wonder how many educators hate what they do but love the schedule and calendar in which they can complain and continue to hate doing it?

I wonder how many educators know that when a child goes off on them or is disrespectful that many times it is built up frustration from how they have been treated by that educator? And let's not forget, most of the stuff they say, probably really is true about the person.

I wonder how many educators reflect on their practices at staff meetings, workshops, or professional development seminars and realize they display some of the same characteristics of the children they educate and trash talk about on a daily basis?

I wonder how many educators who love what they do, actually stand up for the voices who can't speak for themselves because they are muted by threats and intimidation?

I wonder how many educators would want to be taught by themselves if they were their students?

I wonder how many educators would want their children or loved ones taught by someone like them?

I wonder how many educators take into consideration that a few good lesson plans mean nothing to a student who has something called discernment and has figured out you're not in it for the right reasons, and in fact, you celebrate when they're not present?

I wonder how many educators get mad when children are happy they are out, while they pray that certain kids move or never show up again to their class?

I wonder how many educators realize we have an uphill battle? But making a difference everyday can impact people who can then impact even more people.

I wonder how many other educators ask similar questions on a daily basis?

Why Should We Pray?

We should pray because God commands us to pray. God has assured us that when we pray anything in His name that is aligned with His Word and will for our lives, He will answer it. God will never answer a wish but he will answer His Word. God will never answer our emotions because unlike Him, our emotions change. God can and will answer a prayer prayed in faith that will sustain our emotions. It is God's Word that is constant. The Word of God and God are inseparable. Those two are the same yesterday, today, and forever more.

"Is anyone among you suffering? Let him pray. Is anyone cheerful? Let him sing psalms. Is anyone among you sick? Let him call for the elders of the church, and let them pray over him, anointing him with oil in the name of the Lord. And the prayer of faith will save the sick, and the Lord will raise him up. And if he has committed sins, he will be forgiven. Confess your trespasses to one another, and pray for one another, that you may be healed. The effective, fervent prayer of a righteous man avails much. Elijah was a man with a nature like ours, and he prayed earnestly that it would not rain; and it did not rain on the land for three years and six months. And he prayed again, and the heaven gave rain, and the earth produced its fruit."

(Jam. 5:13-18 New King James Version)

"Continue earnestly in prayer, being vigilant in it with thanksgiving;" (Col. 4:2 New King James Version)

"For the eyes of the LORD are on the righteous, And His ears are open to their prayers; But the face of the LORD is against those who do evil." (1 Pet. 3:12 English Standard Version)

"Be anxious for nothing, but in everything by prayer and supplication, with thanksgiving, let your requests be made known to God; and the peace of God, which surpasses all understanding, will guard your hearts and minds through Christ Jesus." (Phil. 4:6-7 New King James Version)

Note to reader: These prayers and devotionals are not meant to be read in a particular order. You can read them as many times as you like in the order that you like. May they bless you, in Jesus' Name.

I thank God, truly, for each and every one of you who will read this book and decide to partner with me and Jesus to pray His will on this earth in the educational arena. May God make your efforts successful. May you increase in wisdom and stature and find favor with God and man. The Lord bless you. The Lord keep you and make His face shine upon you. May the Lord be gracious and kind to you. May the Lord lift up His countenance upon you and give you peace. Your eyes will not go dim and your strength will not fade. You will live a long and prosperous life, in Jesus' name. (Num. 6:24-26, Psalm 90:17, Deut. 34:7).

Declarations and Affirmations

- Every time someone thinks of me, they will speak well of me and give thanks to God for knowing me. (Philippians 1:3)

- I will never slander a current or former employer, employee, co- worker, or colleague. I will not slander and curse my supervisor, boss, manager, team leader, or any other individual God has allowed to work in a leadership position above or over me from the past, present, and future. (Proverbs 30:10)

- I reject the praises of fools today and forever more. (Ecclesiastes 7:5)

- I will never eavesdrop on others, in Jesus' name. (Ecclesiastes 7:21- 22)

- I will never make light of a king or those in authority over me. I will not make fun of those in authority even in the privacy of my own home and bedroom. (Ecclesiastes 10:20)

- I speak with wisdom and I give instructions with kindness. (Proverbs 31:26)

- I listen to counsel and I am not right in my own eyes. (Proverbs 12:15)

- I hate evil and I establish justice in the Educational Gate. The Lord will be gracious unto me. (Amos 5:15)

- I will experience an unexpected encounter with God today so I will never be able to deny Him in my flesh. (Hebrews 13:8)

- I have been granted the key of David. Every door that God has shut, no man can open, and every door that God opens, no man has the power to shut. (Isaiah 22:22)

- I love everything that is right and I hate every false way. (Psalm 119:126)

- I will increase in wisdom and stature. (Luke 2:52)

- The Lord hears me in the time of trouble. His name defends me. God sends me help from the sanctuary and He strengthens me. (Psalm 20:1-2)

- The words of my mouth and the meditations of my heart are acceptable in the eyes of the Lord. The Lord is my strength and He has redeemed me. (Psalm 19:14)

- The Lord rewards me according to my righteousness. The Lord has recompensed me because of the cleanness of my hands. (Psalm 18:20)

- I can run through troops and leap over walls. (Psalm 18:29)

- The Lord has made my feet like hind's feet and has set me upon high places. The Lord continues to teach my hands to war and my fingers to fight. (Psalm 18: 33)

- The Lord is my buckler and shield because I trust in Him. (Psalm 18:30)

- Lord clean me from my secret faults and keep me from my presumptuous sins. These sins do not have dominion over me. (Psalm 119: 12-13)

- I am anointed, the Lord gives me victory, and I trust in the name of the Lord. (Psalm 20: 6)

- My lips speak what is right when I open my mouth. (Proverbs 8:6)

- I am part of the generation that seeks the Lord and seeks the face of the Lord. (Psalm 24:6)

Themed Readings

The Lord gave me two scriptures and one chapter to pray continuously over this now and next generation.

Theme Scriptures

Psalms 24:6

This is Jacob, the generation of those who seek Him, who seek Your face. Selah (King James Version)

Amos 5:15

Hate evil, love good; establish justice in the gate: it may be that the Lord God of hosts Will be gracious to the remnant of Joseph. (New Living Translation)

Amos 5:15

Hate the evil, love the good, and establish judgment in the gate: it may be that the Lord God of hosts will be gracious unto the remnant of Joseph. (King James Version)

Theme Chapter

Psalms 91

Those who live in the shelter of the Most High will find rest in the shadow of the Almighty. This I declare about the Lord. He alone is my refuge, my place of safety; He is my

God, and I trust Him. For He will rescue you from every trap and protect you from deadly disease. He will cover you with His feathers. He will shelter you with His wings. His faithful promises are your armor and protection. Do not be afraid of the terrors of the night, nor the arrow that flies in the day. Do not dread the disease that stalks in darkness, nor the disaster that strikes at midday. Though a thousand fall at your side, though ten thousand are dying around you, these evils will not touch you. Just open your eyes, and see how the wicked are punished. If you make the Lord your refuge, if you make the Most High your shelter, no evil will conquer you; no plague will come near your home. For He will order his angels to protect you wherever you go. They will hold you up with their hands so you won't even hurt your foot on a stone. You will trample upon lions and cobras; you will crush fierce lions and serpents under your feet! The Lord says, "I will rescue those who love Me. I will protect those who trust in My name. When they call on Me, I will answer; I will be with them in trouble. I will rescue and honor them. I will reward them with a long life and give them My salvation. (New Living Translation)

Daily Devotionals

Day 1: Submit to Governing Authorities

"Everyone must submit to governing authorities. For all authority comes from God, and those in positions of authority have been placed there by God. So anyone who rebels against authority is rebelling against what God has instituted, and they will be punished. For the authorities do not strike fear in people who are doing right, but in those who are doing wrong. Would you like to live without fear of the authorities? Do what is right, and they will honor you. The authorities are God's servants, sent for your good. But if you are doing wrong, of course you should be afraid, for they have the power to punish you. They are God's servants, sent for the very purpose of punishing those who do what is wrong. So you must submit to them, not only to avoid punishment, but also to keep a clear conscience." (Rom. 13:1-5 New Living Translation)

Submit to and obey authority and leadership. Regardless of how you feel about them, their personality, or leadership skills, obey authority. If you have a complaint, take it to God. The moment you put your mouth on authority, you become a leper. God has set authority over you and if you aspire to leadership positions or are in leadership, the same word curses you spoke against them will follow you in your position. Be careful of what you say because life and death are indeed in the power of the tongue. Start your year, quarter, month, or week off with a positive attitude regardless of what others around you are saying, doing, or how they are behaving. Remain faithful to God, His leadership, and keep a good attitude.

Day 2: Diligence

"Be diligent to know the state of your flocks, *And* attend to your herds." (Prov. 27:23 New King James Version)

Let your heart have a genuine interest in the students you teach, the young minds you empower, and the souls that are searching for truth. Let your heart have a genuine interest in the people you employ, the people you do business with, the adults you work with, and the people you serve. Care enough to give them truth in all things. Truth starts with the Word of God. I heard Lance Wallnau say, 'Speak Babylonian but think Jesus'. You do not have to quote scripture, chapter and verse, but you can give them a Word that sustains their souls.

Day 3: Do Not Copy the World's Way

"Don't envy violent people or copy their ways. Such wicked people are detestable to the Lord, but he offers his friendship to the godly." (Prov. 3:31-32 New Living Translation)

If you are a new colleague starting a new job, be mindful of the cancerous colleagues who will try and turn you against everyone they have turned against or have turned against them. If you are the cancerous colleague who turns people against one another, pray to God that you will no longer be like that. Turn from following wicked people and their evil ways. If you are neither a new colleague nor a cancerous colleague, find yourself among other co-workers who are pleasant and follow their leadership. Pray for those who are wicked and plot evil plans against the institution, students, colleagues, and/or leadership.

Father in the name of Jesus, open each child's mind to hear and give them the ear of the learned. God help Your children to know that You love them and to not compare themselves to what they see in the mean media world. Help your people, young and old, not compare themselves to what they see in the mean media world. Father help them deal with self- esteem and body image issues. Place positive role models in their lives of your children and your people to help them cope and deal with the pressures of this culture and generation in Jesus Name. Amen.

Day 4: Stay Away from Mockers

"Mockers can get a whole town agitated, but the wise will calm anger." (Prov. 29:8 New Living Translation)

How many of your colleagues do you know who can get the whole team, department, or hallway agitated because of their own issues? Who are you? Are you a mocker or wise educator? How many people are being infected and affected by the poison that is spoken?

Father, help me to command my morning and set the tone, mood, and fellowship of my classroom, office, home, and workplace environment. Father, help me to be a wise educator, and not a mocker. I reject the spirit of mockery, in Jesus' name. Father, I reject and utterly destroy anyone who wants to bring division, turmoil, and chaos to my place of employment or in my business. Father, if it is I who is mocking others and bringing confusion, have mercy on me. Forgive me now and show me a better way. Send good examples my way. Send good examples to my business and to my job. Send good examples to my office. Send good examples to the school districts, and send good examples into my life. Send me colleagues after Your own heart and let me not reject them because of my own issues. In Jesus' name, I pray. Amen.

Day 5: Control Your Anger

Some teachers/educators only care about behavior. Some educators need to become correctional officers or detention officers instead of working in the schools and educational arena. And I would highly suggest that some correctional officers or detention workers who have a heart for change become teachers and work with the youth in the schools. What if I suggested that there are so many students who end up in jail because teachers treat them like they are already incarcerated. Some program the minds of students to think like criminals because the teacher is always suspicious of them and they have to think of ways to get out of trouble and defend themselves before they even do something.

"Fools vent their anger, but the wise quietly hold it back." (Prov. 29:11 New Living Translation)

When students, co-workers, colleagues, or administrators make you upset, you do not have to broadcast it. I know we live in a world where we like to "read" people and give people "the business", but how many of us could stand if God "read us" and gave us "the business". Offended people usually deal with the most rejection. Anger has a sound and speaks. Rejection has a sound and speaks. Unforgiveness and bitterness have their own sounds and they speak. Wisdom has a sound and it speaks. What sound echoes from your vocal cords? What pitch does it make in the spirit? The teachers' lounge and, in some cases, certain classrooms, instead of being a place to relax have become a place of death. Word curses, venting, anger, ungodly sarcasm, slight digs, and hidden jabs are being spewed out. When something goes wrong, you do not have to let everyone know. In fact, a wise person does not mention it. Beyond a classroom, what sounds are heard in your place of employment, business, ministry, heart, and home?

Day 6: No Accusations

"DO not accuse anyone for no reason—when they have done you no harm." (Proverbs 3:30 New International Version)

As an educator, your goal should be to impact the life of a child every day in a positive manner. You should be building each child up. Do not allow what other colleagues tell you about a child to cloud your judgment about them and how you interact with them. Do not allow what your colleagues say about your leadership or other peers to cloud your judgment and make false accusations. As sons and daughters of the King, regardless of your occupation or vocation, you should be striving to impact a group of people in a positive way. Do not allow the thoughts and opinions of others to cloud your judgment.

Day 7: Imitate God

"Imitate, God, therefore, in everything you do, because you are his dear children. Live a life filled with love, following the example of Christ." (Eph. 5:1-2 New Living Translation)

There are three kinds of love that appear in the Bible. Agape love is God's kind of love. Eros love is passionate or sexual love. Phileo is brotherly love. What level of love are you operating from? What credentials do you have to validate your love? Who accredited, confirmed, or approved your love walk? Some people can't relate to God's love because they have never allowed themselves to experience it. Many people have no idea what it means to receive love that you don't have to perform for. Regardless of what you do, not do, say, or not say, God still loves you. When He forgives us for all our sins, it's His love that does that. The tainted relationships we have experienced have ruined God's reputation. Nonetheless, never compare humans to humans and especially never compare a human to God. There is no comparison. Just because a lot of people are agreeing with you doesn't mean you're right and just because a lot of people are disagreeing with you doesn't mean you're wrong. God judges the matter and determines what is right and wrong, what is evil or good, what has evil or good intentions because the information could be true but if the intentions are bad, the message becomes tainted. If we're supposed to love our neighbors as ourselves but we don't love ourselves, how can we then love others? We love them from a broken, rejected, tainted, and hardened heart. Don't do that to people you say you care about. Love them enough to walk away and leave them intact. Or learn to let people walk away from you and leave you intact.

How can you follow an example of someone you do not know? If you're younger and you look to your parents as the example until you can know God for yourself, they are responsible for loving you like Christ. Unfortunately, that is not always the case, but if true believers are loving like Christ, there should be an example around you and if not, start looking. Watch and pray. Ask God to send you someone who displays His agape love.

Day 8: Hate Evil

"You who love the Lord, hate evil! He protects the lives of his godly people and rescues them from the power of the wicked." (Psalm 97:10-12 New Living Translation)

Hate every evil way that you see being exploited and perpetuated in the Educational System. Even if everyone in your department, on your team, in your school, on your job, or in your business, social circle, or within your family are participating and enjoying evil, stay away. Some evil is masked as harmless and ethically correct, but if it is biblically wrong, people are simply enjoying their sin. Regardless of the red tape, bureaucracy, laws, by-laws, and policies set in place, God will indeed rescue those who are godly and live a life that is aimed at pleasing Him. God will surely deliver you from the power of the wicked. The wicked can rule only as long as God allows. If you need to see their wickedness end sooner, start praying for them.

Day 9: Carts of Wickedness

"What sorrow for those who drag their sins behind them with ropes made of lies, who drag wickedness behind them like a cart!" (Isa. 5:18 New Living Translation)

Is your sin or the sins of others so evident and noticeable that people are named by that sin? Has the sin in your life become so habitual, continual, and believable? What about the students you teach? Colleagues? Co-workers, family, friends, and church members? What about other believers? The name that you are currently being called, just may not be the name that heaven knows you by.

Day 10: Ordered Steps

"Allow the Lord to order your steps and direct your path. Do not allow sin, guilt, or an intentional or not offense against God, trap you and keep you from reaching out for help. Do not let anything keep God from being the priority in your life. Ask the Lord to teach you His ways so you can keep His commandments. Allow the Lord to help perfect you so you can copy His behaviors, ideas, and thoughts. That way, your character will truly be a replica of Jesus.

Day 11: No Comparisons

"Pay careful attention to your own work, for then you will get the satisfaction of a job well done, and you won't need to compare yourself to anyone else. For we are each responsible for our own conduct." (Gal. 6:4-5 New Living Translation)

It's ok to be different from the people in your school, on your job, in your businesses, and even in your family who do not have a relationship with God. You should be different so they can ask you what makes you so different. Sometimes we don't have to preach Jesus, but let Jesus on the inside of us preach for us. Other people's perception of you isn't your problem.

Day 12: Hope in God

"We were given this hope when we were saved. If we already have something, we don't need to hope for it. But if we look forward to something we don't yet have, we must wait patiently and confidently. And the Holy Spirit helps us in our weakness. For example, we don't know what God wants us to pray for. But the Holy Spirit prays for us with groanings that cannot be expressed in words." (Rom. 8:24-27 New Living Translation)

When things seem to spin out of control in your school, business, home, office, or workplace, pray to God and wait patiently and confidently. Do not lose hope, but hope in God. When we get weak in the schools or educational arena, ask God to strengthen you. If students have not met the challenge, reached the bar, or complied with expectations, ask the Holy Spirit to pray on your behalf for wisdom, direction, insight, or instructional strategies on how to reach them.

Day 13: Good Judgment

"Leave your simple ways behind, and begin to live; learn to use good judgment." (Prov. 9:6 New Living Translation)

God gave me the revelation one day that some teachers would rather teach dogs than teach the human beings in front of them. I actually talked to a colleague one day after work who told me they preferred animals over teaching the students in their class. Dogs are healthier and love more than people. That might be why more people care about their animals than they do for people; and that just should not be so. God gave us dominion over every creeping, crawling thing. He never said exalt them over mankind.

Have you ever loved God so hard that you failed to love others? Have we loved the Word of God more than people? Think about that. Do you love performance more than you love others? Do you love to be the center of attention rather than sharing the spotlight? Mind you, it's God who gives us the platform.

There have been so many times when people have cared more about how a person looks than the character of their heart and the content of their character and message. Do you know how many are bound right now because we ignore who they are and only see their flesh? How many kids are suffering in silence at school because adults look past their abilities, or lack thereof, to praise another student who is equally intelligent?

Day 14: Record in Heaven

"The LORD is watching everywhere, keeping his eye on both the evil and the good." (Prov. 15:3 New Living Translation)

Remember God's eyes go back and forth watching all the evil and all the good we do. He is that person who goes everywhere with us, sees everything we do, and hears everything we say. What is being recorded in heaven about our lives? I know as an educator, we may sift through the records of students or colleagues from time to time. As a business owner or employee, you may have to check out another person's record or do a background check as part of your responsibilities and roles. However, what does the cumulative folder of our life suggest about us in heaven? What is written about you in the courts of heaven?

Day 15: Remembrance of Me

"Every time I think of you, I give thanks to my God." (Phil. 1:3 Contemporary English Version)

I pray that everyone who remembers me, will speak well of me and give thanks. Allow the Lord to cultivate character in you that brings people peace, joy, and calm. Ask the Lord to remove those things that keep people from connecting with you and building a relationship. Ask the Lord to help you remove the barriers and hindrances in your life that will keep you from desiring to build relationships and connecting with others. May the character of Jesus overtake you and every time people think of you, they will indeed thank God for you.

Day 16: Guide Children

"Direct your children onto the right path, and when they are older, they will not leave it." (Prov. 22:6 New Living Translation)

When students come to you it is because they rely on you to help them, direct them, give them sound advice, and show them the way of their errors. Do not let them down by giving wrong advice and counsel. If you do not have the answer, find out from someone else or direct them to someone who can give them the resolution they are looking for.

If your occupation does not consist of students or children coming to you for help, make sure you are giving wise counsel and advice to those that do. If you do not have the answer, point them to someone who may.

Day 17: New Way of Thinking

"Leave your simple ways behind, and begin to live; learn to use good judgment." (Prov. 9:6 New Living Translation)

Subscribe to the judgment and justice of God. Exchange your mind for the mind of Christ. Exchange your carnal thoughts for the thoughts of God. Since His thoughts are higher than your thoughts, allow His thoughts to supersede your simple ones. Live a life more abundantly when you leave your simple ways behind.

Day 18: Be Fruitful

"Now be fruitful and multiply, and repopulate the earth." (Gen. 9:7 New Living Translation)

As educators, our job is to cultivate the minds of our students so they can go be fruitful, multiply, and help repopulate the earth with other brilliant minds, ensuring that the cycle continues. It all starts with us. We cannot worry about the influences around them, but we can take responsibility for what we teach them. Is what you are teaching something you would want to see duplicated on this earth? Think about your life and how the things you were taught either killed your fruit or helped you become a fruit producer? As educators teaching a myriad of things, we have to be mindful that we are repopulating the earth with people we impact and educate. What legacy will you leave this next and now generation?

Day 19: Righteous Lips

//The lips of the righteous feed many: but fools die for lack of wisdom." (Prov. 10:21 King James)

Have you ever watched any of the "Feed the Hungry" commercials? Have you ever witnessed homeless people on the streets who beg for food? Have you ever witnessed people who have no food looking for it in the most unsanitary places? How does that make you feel? Imagine every time you speak, you are feeding someone something to eat. Are your words prepared and spoken from the most unsanitary places or has it been cleared by spiritual sanitary regulations and FDA rules. Are you feeding students, parents, colleagues, co-workers, bosses, employees, sisters and brothers in Christ, family, friends, and/or foes with righteous words? Do not put yourself in a situation where you will be charged with manslaughter because you killed someone with the words you fed them. Reject being a fool and ask God for wisdom.

Day 20: Defense of the Year

"But the Lord is my defense; and my God is the rock of my refuge." (Psalm 94:22 King James Version)

I have always been taught that defense is what wins the game. If we can keep the opponent from scoring on you, you have a better shot at walking away with a "W". However, you still need to play amazing offense to score on them. In order to score on the enemy, you have to allow God to defend you. The Lord will speak for you, when you can't speak for yourself. Vengeance belongs to God and he judges fairly. Allow Him to be the one you lean into when things are seemingly out of control. When you have been wrongly accused of something and misunderstood, ask the Lord to defend you.

Day 21: Godly Words

"The lips of the godly speak helpful words, but the mouth of the wicked speaks perverse words." (Prov. 10:32 New Living Translation)

What faucet have you drunk from? What do your words taste like when you speak them? Are they refreshing to the soul or are they poisonous to the body? In God, He always presents you with two options. You can choose between good and evil, life and death, and heaven or hell. Are your words godly, helpful, good, and life-giving? Or are they wicked, perverse, hurtful, bitter, evil, and full of death? If the words you spoke and taught to others, especially children, were a direct reflection of their lives, would you be pleased? Have you helped them or harmed them?

Day 22: Wicked Success

"Then I observed that most people are motivated to success because they envy their neighbors. But this, too, is meaningless—like chasing the wind." (Ecclesiastes 4:4)

There is absolutely nothing wrong with success and being successful. God wants us to have life and have it more abundantly. The Lord also said in Jeremiah 17:9 that it was the heart of mankind that was desperately wicked. So, if mankind has wicked hearts, I could infer that mankind innately has wicked intentions. Once the Lord cleanses the heart, the intentions shall also be cleansed. Being jealous of others will leave your soul sick. Do not allow the success of others to bring turmoil or disappointment to your life. While you are busy watching someone else, they are busy working on the dreams and goals that God has placed inside them. Allow every success you have with children, students, within the educational arena, sports arena, medical arena, or any other sphere of influence you have, to be genuine. Let every success that comes from interacting with other adults, family, friends, business partners, or ministries, be rooted in God. You will enjoy the success and accomplishment more because you will know the satisfaction you felt came from your own motivation and drive and not a secret jealousy you had for someone else. Out do the best you from yesterday.

Day 23: Favor from God

"In the sixth month of Elizabeth's pregnancy, God sent the angel Gabriel to Nazareth, a village in Galilee, to a virgin named Mary. She was engaged to be married to a man named Joseph, a descendant of King David. Gabriel appeared to her and said, "Greetings, favored woman! The Lord is with you!" (Luke 1:26-28 New Living Translation)

Whether you are male or female, God is with you. You are pregnant with the promises of God and He expects you to carry them for the full term. If the school year is the full term in which you are to carry what God has given you, are you properly nourishing it? Your students are pregnant with the promises of God. Are you properly nourishing them? If you are not an educator in the school system, you are still an educator in your respective area. Are you properly nourishing the students, the adults, the patients, the clients, the parishioners, the children, the followers, fans, and foes God has placed you in charge to take care of. Are you carrying them full term or have you aborted them like the millions of babies Planned Parenthood has assisted in aborting?

Day 24: Lazy People

"Lazy people want much but get little, but those who work hard will prosper." (Proverbs 13:4 New Living Translation)

When you come to work, work. If you are supposed to be planning, plan. If you are supposed to be meeting, be productive in the meeting. If you are supposed to be at work at a set time, be on time. Perfect your craft and be the best educator you can be. Be the best business owner you can be. Be the best you, you can be.

Day 25: Love One Another

"Dear friends, let us continue to love one another, for love comes from God. Anyone who loves is a child of God and knows God. But anyone who does not love does not know God, for God is love." (1 John 4:7-8 New Living Translation)

Loving others can make you feel warm and fuzzy on the inside. Allow the love of God to engulf your entire being. Allow the love of God to serenade you and draw you to Him. God is love. When you display the attributes and characteristics of love, you have become God in the flesh. Love people when it hurts. Love people when they do not deserve it. Love people when they avenge you. Love people when they mistreat or mishandle you. God did that for you. Love the students you teach, the children you have, the family you were born to or raised in. Love the ministry you serve in, the neighborhood you live in, the employers you have and the colleagues you work with. Be the difference maker today in someone's life. It was that same goodness that drew us to God. Allow others to experience the love you received by showing it to them and drawing them closer to Him.

Day 26: Anger That Settles

"Instead, let the Spirit renew your thoughts and attitudes. Put on your new nature, created to be like God—truly righteous and holy. So stop telling lies. Let us tell our neighbors the truth, for we are all parts of the same body. And "don't sin by letting anger control you." Don't let the sun go down while you are still angry, for anger gives a foothold to the devil." (Eph. 4:23-27 New Living Translation)

There are times when we feel like we must be dishonest, but that is the most dishonest lie you can tell yourself. Deliverance made easy occurs when you stop doing something. If you lie, stop it. If you cheat, stop it. If you wrongly accuse others, stop it. Whatever you are doing that is contrary to the Word and will of God, stop it. If you need additional help and support, ask the Lord to direct you to the right people. We all sin and fall short of the glory of God. God has uniquely created us all and has hard wired us with emotions. Anger is one emotion that if left unchecked and unmonitored, can cause traumatic damage. Anger is a healthy emotion when dealt with properly. Confront issues and do not allow them to settle in your heart and cause you to burn with anger and revenge. When you remain angry, all kinds of ungodly thoughts start to drive your actions.

Deal with the anger in a godly and righteous way so you can have a godly and righteous outcome. Renew your way of thinking and act in God's way, so you can have godly and holy outcomes.

Day 27: Right Path

"Direct your children onto the right path, and when they are older, they will not leave it." (Prov. 22:6 New Living Translation)

As parents, caretakers, guardians, role models, or educators, you are responsible for directing children to the right path. Who determines the right path for a child? Who approves the right path for children? The Lord has provided a blueprint and guide in the Word of God for each person's life, starting from the time they are conceived until the time they die. The Lord is the one who approves the path that one must take. Even if you do not agree with the right path, if the Lord says it in his Word, do not stand in the way. If you are pointing and directing them to the right path as children, when they get older, they will travel that same path. Even if they veer off the path, they will remember how to find it again, or they will at least know how to ask for directions to get back on it. If you are responsible for children whose path has not been rightly directed, help and guide them. If you do not know how to guide them, ask someone else who can. Pray to God to send people in their lives to guide them. Be patient with them while they get acclimated to a new path. Children need guidance and they need to be taught. Teach them. If their path has been rightly directed, do not provide other options that would deter them. Do not allow others to provide options even for you that would deter you from your right path.

Day 28: Own Opinions

"Fools have no interest in understanding; they only want to air their own opinions." (Prov. 18:2 New Living Translation)

As an educator or parent, be open to what children have to say. There should not be only one right way to do something in your class or home. Of course, there is protocol and order, but be open to taking suggestions from others, on how to make your classroom, office, or workspace more pleasant and appealing, especially the children. Do not be so quick to shut others down because you do not necessarily agree with them. Hear them out and if it is something that does not go against your moral and ethical standards, try it.

Day 29: Delight of Kings

"Righteous lips are the delight of kings; and they love him that speaketh right." (Proverbs 16:13 King James Version)

"The king is pleased with words from righteous lips; he loves those who speak honestly." (Prov. 16:13 New Living Translation)

Be honest in all that you say and do. Speak with integrity to your students and model for them how they should speak to you. The King which is the Lord God Almighty will be pleased with you, but your local leadership and "king" will also take notice. Be to them what you want them to be to you. The highest spiritual authority overrides the greatest secular authority any given day. Walk in your authority while being submitted and under authority.

Day 30: 20/20 Vision

"Then the Lord answered me and said: "Write the vision and make it plain on tablets, that he may run who reads it." (Habakkuk 2:2 New King James Version)

Make the vision very clear in your classroom so each student can run after it and obtain it. If they miss the mark, redirect and guide them so they can continue to run for success. After you have written the vision, make sure it is easy for them to access and understand. Make the vision very clear in your life, your home, your business, your family, and your ministry. Under the direction of The Holy Spirit, draw a blueprint for your life and allow God to be the chief architect. We can make all the plans we like, but it is God who gives the right answers. Seek his counsel for your answers.

Day 31: Help Me Lord

"Unless the Lord had been my help, my soul had almost dwelt in silence." (Psalm 94:17 King James Version)

When life seems to get the best of you, ask the Lord to help you. Go back to the recesses of your mind and think of a time when you know it was only God who helped you. Think back to a time when you know that it was God who overturned a guilty verdict in your life. You may have been guilty of lying. You may have been guilty of manipulation. You may have been guilty of wrong motives and intentions. You may have been guilty of sinning, but God helped you. Think back to a time when God helped you and you didn't even ask for His help or wanted it. Think back to a time when God did not allow your soul to remain silent, but you broke out in praise and you were able to testify. That same God is the same one who is going to help you today. If you need help with your children, your students, adults, or help with balancing your own life, God is ready to help you. Do not be surprise when He sends someone who has the gifts to help you. It may be in the form of a child or someone you least expect, but do not reject the help He is sending.

Prayers for Educators

Prayer for Salvation

If you're going to be saved, be saved for real. Count the cost of salvation and make a decision. It's a hard decision because you lose tangible things that include people, but you gain something much more valuable. We can't pick and choose what sins we like and which ones we don't. There are no levels in sin. The penalty of them all is death. But when you make Jesus the Lord of all, He replaces death with eternal life. We want the promises of God but we don't want to meet the conditions. Many people say you can't tell them whom to love, but you sure can tell them if it's right or wrong. You surely can tell them if it's biblical or not.

Don't level off sin. It's all wrong, but Jesus is so compassionate for his people. Receive forgiveness and live. Do not reject forgiveness and commit suicide. There is nothing that we have done that will turn God away from us. Once we return to God, He will forget it like it never happened. *Psalms 103:12* declares, *"He has removed our sins as far from us as the east is from the west."* (New Living Translation)

Romans 10:9 assures you, *"...if you confess with your mouth that Jesus is Lord and believe in your heart that God raised him from the dead, you will be saved"* (English Standard Version). It is the goodness of God that makes us repent. Indeed, our defense is God, but Psalm 7:11 also asserts that God is angry with the wicked all day. I opted to allow God to be my defense because I often remember how merciful, kind, and long suffering He has been and still is to me. When I thought about all the times I should have opened my eyes in hell, but God spared my life, it was enough to make me repent. God is love and He loves us so much that He does not want us to end up in eternal damnation. If you desire to be saved and this is not an emotional "high" or "feeling", you can repeat the following prayer and ask Him to save you. If you are a backslider who once knew God but slid out of His will, you do know He is married to you, right? We are given clear instructions in *Jeremiah 3:14: "Return, O backsliding children," says the Lord; "for I am married to you. I will take you, one from a city and two from a family, and I will bring you to Zion"* (New King James Version).

Father, in the name of Jesus, I come to You and ask that You save me. I repent for everything I have done that was not pleasing to You, but may have been pleasing to me and to others. Father, please forgive me and save me. I want You to be Lord and Savior in my life. I do not know what all of this means and how it will all turn out, but I am trusting You. I am walking by faith and not by what I see and not by what I feel at this moment. Give me a grace to obey You and give me daily bread and daily instruction. Father, assure and reassure me that You have heard me and that You have signed my name in the Lamb's Book of Life. I know salvation is the first step, so please lead me every day. Give me the ability to read the Word of God which is the Bible and to study to show myself approved. God help me to make right choices and display godly behaviors. All of this is new for me but I want to experience a newness in my life. I have tried and did a lot of things that have failed. I know that there is no failure in You. I want to be saved and I want to be a follower of You. Lead me and I shall follow. According to Psalm 119:33 "Guide my steps by your word, so I will not be overcome by evil. Ransom me from the oppression of evil people; then I can obey your commandments." (New Living Translation). Look upon me with love; teach me Your decrees. Rivers of tears gush from my eyes because people disobey your instructions, and I was one who obeyed Your instructions. I disobeyed them many times knowing it was wrong, but I ask for forgiveness now. I want to obey Your instructions. Thank You for sending Your Son, Jesus, to die for me and redeem me back to You. Thank You for loving me so much. Father, help me serve You for the rest of my life, for I desire to please You in all of my ways. Thank You that You never left me and You never abandoned me even if I felt like You did. Thank You for every test, trial, and every testimony that I shall share about Your goodness. Thank You for loving me when I felt unlovable.

Thank You for loving me when I did not love me and did not feel worthy of anyone else loving me. Thank You because You know my goings and comings. You know the very intent of my heart. You see all the evil and good that I do, and You still love me. I love You, Father, and I know there are consequences to sin, but I thank You for forgiving me of mine and receiving me as Your child. I pray this in Jesus' Name.

Amen

Prayer of Exaltation

Father, help me bump into You this morning as I pray and petition heaven. I know that You answer my prayers before I even finish praying, but before I ask You for anything, I want to exalt and adore You. You are alpha and omega. You are the lover of my soul and the lover of justice. You are the bright morning star. You are the breath that I am currently breathing. You are my alarm clock. You are the God of peace and restoration, as You are the God of war and the mightiest warrior. Fight for me this morning, Lord. You are the Rose of Sharon, Jehovah Shalom, Jehovah Sabaoth. You are the Lord of Hosts. You are my buckler, creator, ancient of days, refining fire, Almighty God, Creator of Israel, deliverer, my dwelling place, and the God who sees. Lord, Your eyes go to and fro watching all the evil and all the good I do. You are Everlasting God, Everlasting King, Father of Lights and never the father of lies. You are the same yesterday, today, and forevermore. You are my fortress, the fountain of living waters that never run dry. You are my hiding place, my high tower, and the horn of my salvation. You are my banner, my judge, my king, and my keeper. Father, You are the lawgiver, the living God, the God who heals, and the God who reigns forever and ever. You are my shelter, my shepherd, my strength, and my shield. You are my portion, my potter, my rock, and my wall of fire.

Son of God, You are my advocate. You are Almighty, the Anointed One, Banner for the Nations, Bishop of my Soul, Bridegroom, Branch of Righteousness, Bread, and Captain of my Salvation. Jesus, you are the Chief Cornerstone, Chosen of God, Commander of the Army of the Lord, Dayspring from on High, Desire of All Nations, Door, Emmanuel, Faithful, and Everlasting Light. Son of Man, you are Governor, High Priest, Horn of my Salvation, Lamb of God, Last Adam, Lion of the Tribe of Judah, Lord of Peace, Lord of the Harvest, Master, Mediator, Messiah, and The Only Wise God. I call you Physician, Prince, Redeemer, Teacher, The Way, The Truth, and The Life. Jesus, I pray in Your name now.

Holy Spirit come and when You come, do not be silent. Holy Spirit come, and when You come, do not be silent. You are my advocate, spirit of truth, Eternal spirit, Counselor, Free Spirit, Holy One, New Spirit, Spirit of Compassion and Might, Spirit of Faith, and Spirit of Glory. You are My Answerer, Paraclete, Spirit of Prophecy, Spirit of Revelation, Knowledge and Understanding, and Spirit of Truth. Holy Ghost come, and when You come, do not be silent.

Father, help me hate evil, love good and establish justice in the educational arena and marketplace. I am establishing justice today in the educational arena and the justice that we establish, in Jesus's name, cannot be overthrown and it cannot be shaken. The government is upon Your shoulders and I call You Wonderful Counselor, Mighty God, Everlasting Father, Prince of Peace. Your government and Your peace will never end. You rule with fairness and justice from the throne of David for all eternity. The passionate commitment of the Lord of Heaven's Armies will make this happen. Father release Heaven's Armies to fight on behalf of the educational system. Father I know that when people of God come together to pray, great and miraculous things can and do happen. You said in *Isaiah 65:23-24 "They shall not labor in vain, nor bring forth for trouble; for they are the seed of the blessed of the Lord, and their offspring with them. And it shall come to pass, that before they call, I will answer; and while they are yet speaking, I will hear"*. Abba Father I know that you hear me and I know that is you who answers me. Thank You, Jesus. Thank You, Abba for answering me and turning things around. Thank You that my labor is not in vain. Father, You know my struggles, issues, hang-ups, and areas of need even before I mention them to You. Answer the secret things of my heart this today, work related and non-work related. Thank You, Jesus, that You were the greatest teacher that ever lived and You are our greatest example of an educator. Help me Jesus. Give me this day my daily bread and forgive my sins, as I have forgiven those who sin against me. Please don't let me yield to temptation, but rescue me from the evil one.

Father, help me not be unified just in occupation or commonalities, but let me be unified in the spirit with other believers praying for the educational system. I create a circuit in the spirit with those praying to shatter hell and glorify the kingdom of light. I am a kingdom dweller and kingdom citizen. Father, in JESUS' name, I ask for wisdom, knowledge, and understanding for every intercessor today. Give me the ears of the learned. Help me to be as wise as a serpent but harmless as a dove. Help me to believe Your Word and step out on faith. Help me Jesus. Father, in JESUS' name, I bind all demons of infirmity, sickness, disease, and illnesses.

I loose myself and others from these demons and I loose the healing virtue of JESUS Christ into our bodies. Children are well. Colleagues are well. Administrators are well. Superintendents are well. Principals are well. Coaches, specialists, mentors, counselors, professors, admission counselors' therapist, and every employee and employer that is working in the educational arena is well in mind, body, and soul. Raise our level of faith today. Raise our level of faith today. Raise our level of faith today in Jesus Name.

Amen

Prayer for Protection

Father, according to *Ephesians 6:13-18*, I put on the whole armor of God today and I keep it on. I put on the belt of truth. My shoes are full of peace that surpasses all understanding. My peace is the peace that You give, oh Mighty God. I have on the shield of faith. My faith is in You and it's my hope of things that I do not see but I am hoping for. My head is covered and protected with salvation. I carry Your sword which is Jesus who has manifested into flesh from Your Word. Thank You, Holy Spirit for dwelling on the inside of me and I repent now for grieving You by the way I may have lived or live. Lead me all in truth and help me walk this walk out. I cannot do it alone but I are leaning and trusting on You. Father, I know You hear my prayers and I am confident that You will answer. Thank You, Jesus for Your blood on the cross that saved all humanity. Receive me into Your kingdom to be a servant of You now. Fill and refill me with Your Holy Spirit. I will always pray and make supplication to You in the Spirit. I pray *Zechariah 9:12* over my life and the life of my children now. I have come back to the place of safety in You. As a prisoner of Christ, I still have hope in You. You have promised that You will repay me with two blessings for each of my troubles. I believe it and I receive it now, in Jesus' name. I love You for who You are and all that You have and will do. You are the same in my past, my present, and my future according to *Hebrews 13:8*. Father God, give me an unexpected encounter with You today so I will never be able to deny You in my flesh again. Regulate my mind now to hear from You. I need You, Lord. I have to go in Your strength because I cannot do it on our own. Carry me when I am weak. Pull me when I don't move, and push me when I am too afraid.

I come against every Satanic and demonic altar that has been erected by some entity other than the one and only true and living God, on my behalf. Every witch in operation over my life must die by the fire of God now. Snuff out every snake in my life with the sulfur You have reserved for the lake of burning fire. I send confusion back on the one who has sent confusion to my mind. I send jealousy back to the one who has set jealousy in my path. I send wickedness and lewdness back on the perverse one now in Jesus' mighty name. Thank you for protecting me. Thank you for protecting my family. Thank you for protecting my friends and my foes in Jesus Name. Thank you that your name protects all that concerns me. Thank you for divine protection wherever I go in Jesus Name.

Amen

Prayer for A Burden to Pray

Father, Your word says in 2 Samuel 7:28-29, *"For You are God, O Sovereign Lord. Your words are truth, and You have promised these good things to Your servant. And now, may it please You to bless the house of Your servant, so that it may continue forever before You. For You have spoken, and when You grant a blessing to Your servant, O Sovereign Lord, it is an eternal blessing!" (New Living Translation).* Father God, I am asking that You bless me, bless my family, bless my spiritual family, and bless everyone who will unite to pray for this educational system. I plead the blood of Jesus over us now and over our children. May You place a hedge of protection over our seed, seeds, and our wombs. I ask that You place a blood shield and a blood wall around our children, and our children to come, as they go and come daily. Protect them while they are in school. Protect them while they are on their jobs, and protect them while they are at home. Keep this generation safe. According to *Psalm 24:6*, this is the generation that seeks You, this is the generation that seeks Your face. Protect us daily while we are working, while we are on our jobs, while we are traveling, while these children are in school, and while we are in our homes. Father help us unite in the spirit with one another and give us a burden to pray to You. You said You would heal our land if we turn away from our sins. 2 Chronicles 7:14 declares *"...if My people who are called by My name humble themselves and pray and seek My face and turn from their wicked ways, I will hear from heaven and will forgive their sins and heal their land"* *(English Standard Version).* Father, shine Your light on us today and help us to repent to You and turn from our wicked ways. Show us our errors so we can turn from them. I want to please You, Lord. I want to serve you, Lord. I want to live for You wholeheartedly, Father. Thank You, Jesus, for interceding on my behalf to the Father. Father help me listen to the words of the wise and apply instruction to my heart, according to Proverbs 22:17.

Amen

Prayer for Intercessors Praying for the Educational System

Father, thank you that You will give of the Holy Spirit that is upon me to pray for this generation and place it on everyone else who will read this book. Father, let us all bear the burden of the people and the school system so that we will not bear this alone. You looked down from the height of Your sanctuary; from heaven and Lord you have viewed the earth. You hear the groaning of the prisoners. Father as you look down and view this earth, raise up individuals one by one who will begin to intercede and pray for this academic and educational system. You have designated a time to release those appointed to death. You have designated a time to declare the name of the Lord in Zion, and your praise in Jerusalem, and the educational arena. May you place a burning desire on the inside of each one of us to pray daily for this academic system. Father, I speak *Psalm 102:28* over this generation. You said the children of your people will live in security. Thank you for allowing your children to live in security. You said their children's children will thrive in your presence and I thank you in advance for them thriving. Jesus I bless Your name with all of my soul.

Amen

Prayer for Educators with Pure Hearts

E ven as you are with me, Father, be with everyone who is standing in the gap for our children, the youth of this world, and this next and now generation. Father, according to *Psalm 24:6*, this is Jacob, the generation of those who seek Him, who seek Your face. Selah.

Your Word says in *Psalm 24:1-5 "The earth is the Lord's, and all its fullness, The world and those who dwell therein. For He has founded it upon the seas, And established it upon the waters. Who may ascend into the hill of the Lord? Or who may stand in His holy place? He who has clean hands and a pure heart, Who has not lifted up his soul to an idol, Nor sworn deceitfully. He shall receive blessing from the Lord, And righteousness from the God of his salvation."* (New King James Version)

Father, I am asking now that You wash my heart and clean my hands so I can receive the blessings that You have for me. Wash my heart and clean my hands so I can stand before You and Your people to proclaim Your Word. Wash my heart so I can proclaim that You have come to rescue the afflicted and persecuted within the educational system. I am not asking for a tangible blessing, but a blessing of favor upon my life to do what it is You have called me to do in this earth. Father, I ask that You wash my co-laborers' hearts and clean their hands so they can be fitted properly to receive every blessing You have for them. *Psalm 51:1-2* declares *"Have mercy upon me, O God, According to Your lovingkindness; According to the multitude of Your tender mercies, Blot out my transgressions. Wash me thoroughly from my iniquity, And cleanse me from my sin."* (New King James Version)

Father, help me teach Your children not to envy evil people or desire their company as Your Word says in *Proverbs 24:1.* Give me wisdom on how to wage war in the educational system. Give me insight, knowledge, and understanding on how to overcome the plots and plans of the evil doers. Shake out every witch, sorcerer, sooth-sayer, wizard, and evil one from the educational system. Relocate these individuals to other places of employment. Turn their hearts away from teaching and turn it to serving their own god of this world. I do not permit a sorceress to live as You do not permit a sorceress to live according to *Exodus 22:18.* Reroute administrators, educators, teachers, and coaches who seek harm and evil in their hearts for children. Every pedophile, every molester, every word curser, and every adult who speaks evil of children, Father let them not teach in the upcoming year. *Matthew 19:14* says that You, Jesus, called them to *Him* and said, *"Let the little children come to Me, and do not forbid them; for of such is the kingdom of heaven."* (New King James Version)

Amen

Prayer for Victory

So, Father God, I ask now in Your proper time, You judge uprightly. Father, I know that promotion comes from You and I am asking that You sit down the wicked and evil ones in the educational systems. Father, I am asking now that You shake out the evil doers that stretch across every arena connected and related to the educational system. When You exalt the righteous, Father, help me not use Your platform or power for evil or compromise, but for Your glory. Do it for Your name's sake.

Psalm 23: 1-3 boasts that You, Lord, *are* my shepherd; I shall not want. You make and continually make me to lie down in green pastures. You lead and continually lead me beside the still waters. You have restored, You are restoring me right now, and will forever restore our souls. You have lead and will lead me as You are leading me now in the paths of righteousness for Your name's sake. Yahweh will be glorified. Elohim will be glorified. Jehovah Jireh will be glorified. Jehovah Tsidkenu will be glorified. The Lord of Hosts will be glorified. El Shaddai will be glorified. Master Teacher will be glorified. Yahweh Shammah will be glorified. Yahweh Sabaoth will be glorified. The Son of God, the Lion of the Tribe of Judah, the one who reigns over the just and unjust will be glorified. Jesus, You will be glorified.

The one Who the elders cry Holy, Holy, Holy in the Book of Revelation will be glorified. A mighty chorus sings in *Revelation 5: 12 "...Worthy is the Lamb who was slain to receive power, and riches, and wisdom, and strength and honor, and glory, and blessing."* (King James Version)

"Yea, though I walk through the valley of the shadow of death, I will fear no evil; For You *are* with me; Your rod and Your staff, they comfort me. You prepare a table before me in the presence of our enemies; You anoint my head with oil; My cup runs over. Surely goodness and mercy shall follow me all the days of my life; and I will dwell in the house of the Lord forever." (Psalm 23:1-6 New International Version - *Adaptation*)

Let me not pray amiss or pray my emotions, but I pray Your Word because it is Your Word that You hasten over to perform.

"The words of Jeremiah the son of Hilkiah, of the priests who *were* in Anathoth in the land of Benjamin, to whom the word of the Lord came in the days of Josiah the son of Amon, king of Judah, in the thirteenth year of his reign. It came also in the days of Jehoiakim the son of Josiah, king of Judah, until the end of the eleventh year of Zedekiah the son of Josiah, king of Judah, until the carrying away of Jerusalem captive in the fifth month. Then the word of the

Lord came to me, saying: "Before I formed you in the womb I knew you; Before you were born I sanctified you; I ordained you a prophet to the nations." Then said I: "Ah, Lord God! Behold, I cannot speak, for I *am* a youth." But the Lord said to me: "Do not say, 'I *am* a youth,' For you shall go to all to whom I send you, And whatever I command you, you shall speak. Do not be afraid of their faces, For I *am* with you to deliver you," says the Lord. Then the Lord put forth His hand and touched my mouth, and the Lord said to me: "Behold, I have put My words in your mouth. See, I have this day set you over the nations and over the kingdoms, To root out and to pull down, To destroy and to throw down, To build and to plant." Moreover the word of the Lord came to me, saying, "Jeremiah, what do you see?" And I said, "I see a branch of an almond tree." Then the Lord said to me, "You have seen well, for I am ready to perform My word." And the word of the Lord came to me the second time, saying, "What do you see?" And I said, "I see a boiling pot, and it is facing away from the north." Then the Lord said to me: "Out of the north calamity shall break forth on all the inhabitants of the land. For behold, I am calling All the families of the kingdoms of the north," says the Lord; "They shall come and each one set his throne at the entrance of the gates of Jerusalem, Against all its walls all around, And against all the cities of Judah. I will utter

My judgments against them concerning all their wickedness, Because they have forsaken Me, Burned incense to other gods, And worshiped the works of their own hands. "Therefore prepare yourself and arise, And speak to them all that I command you. Do not be dismayed before their faces, Lest I dismay you before them. For behold, I have made you this day A fortified city and an iron pillar, And bronze walls against the whole land— Against the kings of Judah, Against its princes, Against its priests, And against the people of the land. They will fight against you, But they shall not prevail against you, For I am with you," says the Lord, "to deliver you." (Jeremiah 1:1-11 New King James Version)

Amen

Prayer for Defeat Over Our Enemies

Father, let the wicked be overthrown by their mouth. God let the wicked fall because they do not seek counsel. Father, let the merciful do good for their own soul, but he who is cruel trouble their own flesh. The wicked man does deceptive work, but he who sows righteousness will have a sure reward. Father, as I sow righteousness, let me have a sure reward with You in heaven and on earth. I know righteousness leads to life, and I will not be evil and pursue my own death. Father, You said those who are of a perverse heart are an abomination to the LORD, but the blameless in their ways are Your delight. Though they join forces, the wicked will not go unpunished; but the posterity of the righteous will be delivered. So, Father, I thank You that the wickedness in the schools will not go unpunished but You will deliver right punishment and justice. Continue to help Your righteous people to do only good so they can seek favor, and let those who seek evil find trouble in Jesus Name.

Amen

Prayer for Success

According to Psalm 90:17 may the Lord my God show me his approval and make my efforts successful. Yes, make my efforts successful! Father, may you bless me. May you keep me. May you make your face shine upon me, and be gracious unto me. May you Lord lift up Your countenance upon me, and give me peace. And I shall put Your name upon the children of Israel, upon the children I teach and the children I have, and You will bless them in Jesus Name. May a glory cloud show up in the schools across America this day. May a glory cloud show up in the classrooms across the nation this day. May a glory cloud show up in offices today. May a glory cloud show up in my office or place of employment today in Jesus' name. May a glory cloud show up in stores, factories, businesses, ministries, churches, and everywhere I go today. I speak this over this nation today in Jesus' name. I speak life into dead situations. I say arise, in Jesus' name. Arise, in Jesus' name. Arise, in Jesus' Name.

Amen

Prayer for Promotion

So, Father God, I ask now in Your proper time, You judge uprightly. Father, I know that promotion does not come from the east or the west, but it comes from You. As you did with Joseph, may I find favor in your sight. May you place me in leadership to carry out your plans in this earth. When You exalt me as your righteous one, Father help me not use my platform or power for evil or compromise, but for your glory. Do it for Your name sake. No man or woman can take the credit; for this is Your doing and it is marvelous in Your sight. I give You all the glory and I give You all the adoration. For it is You who answers by fire. It is You who speaks like thunder. It is You who releases snow from Your treasury in heaven. It is You, God, who is the sovereign and holy one. I love you and honor you. I bless your name and I thank you in advance. Thank you for answering this prayer in Jesus Name.

Amen

Prayers For Employers And Employees In The Educational System

Prophetic Scripture for The Educational System

Based on *Ezekiel 11:1-25*, "Then the Spirit picked me up and took me to the gate of the Temple that faces east. There were twenty-five men standing at the gate. I recognized the leaders, Jaazaniah son of Azzur and Pelatiah son of Benaiah. God said, 'Servant of God, these are the men who draw up blueprints for sin, who think up new programs for evil in this city. They say, "We can make anything happen here. We're the best. We're the choice pieces of meat in the soup pot." 'Oppose them, servant of God. Preach against them.' Then the Spirit of God came upon me and told me what to say: This is what God says: That's a fine public speech, leaders and lawmakers, but I know what you are thinking. You've murdered a lot of people in this city and within the educational system. The streets are piled high with corpses. Therefore, this is what God, the Master, says: The corpses that you've piled in the streets and in the school systems are the meat and your cities are the soup pot, and *you're* not even in the pot! I'm throwing you out! You fear war, but war is what you're going to get. I'm bringing war against you. I'm throwing you out of your cities and educational systems, giving you over to foreigners, and punishing you good. You'll be killed in battle. I'll carry out judgment on you at the borders of Israel. Then you'll realize that I am God. <u>Your cities and the school systems</u> will not be your soup pot and you won't be the choice pieces of meat in it either. Hardly. I will carry out judgment on you at the borders of Israel and you'll realize that I am God, for you haven't followed my statutes and ordinances. Instead of following My ways, you've sunk to the level of the laws of the nations <u>and other educational systems and districts</u> around you. Even while I was preaching, Pelatiah son of Benaiah died. I fell down, face to the ground, and prayed loudly, "O Master, God! Will you completely wipe out what's left of Israel?" The answer from God came back: <u>Servant of God</u>, your brothers—I mean the whole people of Israel who are in exile with you—are the people of whom the citizens of Jerusalem are saying, 'They're in the far country, far from God. This land has been given to us to own.' Well, tell them this, 'This is your message from God, the Master. True, I sent you to the far country, <u>to various schools, districts, and</u> <u>arenas in the educational field</u> and scattered you through other lands, <u>towns, cities, states, and countries</u>. All the same, I've provided you a temporary sanctuary in the countries, <u>towns, cities, states, districts, and systems where you've gone</u>. I will gather you back from those countries and lands where you've been scattered and give you back the land of Israel. You'll come back and clean house, throw out all the rotten images and obscene idols. I'll give you a new heart. I'll put a new spirit in you. I'll cut out your stone heart and replace it with a red-blooded, firm-muscled heart. Then you'll obey my statutes and be careful to obey my commands. You'll be My people! I'll be your God! But not those who are self-willed and addicted to their rotten images and obscene idols! I'll see that they're paid in full for what they've done. Decree of God, the Master. Then the cherubim spread their wings, with the wheels beside them and the Glory of the God of Israel hovering over them. The Glory of God ascended from within the city and rested on the mountain to the east of the city. Then, still in the vision given me by the Spirit of God, the Spirit took me and carried me back to the exiles in Babylon. And then the vision left me. I told the educators everything that was written in God's Word.

Revelation About Educators and Correctional Officers

(12/15/16 11:02 am) The Holy Spirit spoke to me while I was in my classroom.

Some teachers and educators only care about behavior. Some educators need to become correctional officers or detention officers instead of working in the schools and educational arena. And I would highly suggest that some correctional officers or detention workers who have a heart for change become teachers and work with the youth in the schools. What if I suggested that there are so many students who end up in jail because teachers treat them like they are already incarcerated. Some program the minds of students to think like criminals because the teacher is always suspicious of them, and they have to think of ways to get out of trouble and defend themselves before they have even done anything.

Prayer for Administrators

Father, I lift up every administrator that serves as a leader in the educational system. Every administrator who oversees the well-being, infrastructure, and day-to-day operations of an academic facility, program, idea, or business; I lift them up to You, now. Father, may You bless them and satisfy them with good things. May they never lack any good thing and may they fear You and honor You. Father, purify them and wash their hearts now. Drive out anything in them that will hinder them from performing the way You want them to perform. Wash their hearts and give them Your heart. Allow them to lead with excellence and fairness. May each administrator be gentle, kind, patient, and loving. May they execute business with a professional, yet Christ-like, manner. According to Your word in *Romans 13:1*, may those whom they govern, submit to them. Father, I thank You for Your administrators because I know that all positions of authority have come from You. Even if I want to retaliate, be upset, or complain, help me submit to my administrators and those in authority with a loving heart. May I bring my complaints to You. Teach Your administrators how to lead with love, serve with excellence, and display integrity at all times. May the love of Jesus Christ exude out of their hearts today in Jesus Name.

Amen

Prayer for Teachers and Professors

Jesus is the greatest teacher alive and I pray that every teacher in this nation seek to be Christ-like. Father, give them the grace to teach well. Allow them to give instruction with kindness and allow them to be respected by their peers, colleagues, administrators, parents, and students. Father, may every teacher give instruction accurately and with clarity. May their speech be articulate and their faith be strong in You. Father, every wrong motive and every hidden agenda that is in the heart of a teacher, may it be exposed now. Your eyes go to and fro throughout this earth, and You see all the evil and all the good we do. Every witch that is employed as a teacher in the educational system, I stand on *Exodus 22:18* and drive them out now. They will not operate, thrive, or, work in the schools with our children. Father, let every sexual predator be exposed now. Every teacher who desires harm to come upon these children, may You escort them out of the educational arena today, in Jesus' name. Every teacher who does not know and has rebelled against You, may You raise up other godly teachers to minister to them. May those who have been called and chosen by You, repent and be saved by Your grace. Every teacher who desires to grow and become better, send them help from the sanctuary. Send them mentors, colleagues, and other teachers to help strengthen their craft and perfect their imperfections. Every teacher who has a heart for the children, may You send the Holy Ghost to blow a fresh wind into their entire being. May they be revived by You, in Jesus' name. May fresh ideas, creative projects, and rigorous and fun strategies come upon them now. May every righteous teacher excel above their peers and reach children that no other colleague can reach. May their impact be lasting and residual. May each child that they have positively impacted, come back and bless them. May they receive gifts, bonuses, money, and adoration that they never expected and never sought after. May they be honored for the work they do in Jesus Name. *(Psalm 141:2-3, Rom. 12:6-7 New Living Translation)*

Amen

Prayer for Bus Drivers

Father, I am praying for every bus driver today. I lift them up to You. Let them know they are loved, valuable, and a huge asset to what takes place in school daily. I speak peace, joy, longsuffering, gentleness, patience, kindness, goodness, faithfulness, and self-control into their lives. Every time they have been made to feel inadequate and less important, Father, shatter those negative and ill spoken words off of their lives today. Father, I honor them and love them. Let them know that. Help us all appreciate every bus driver today. Father thank you for allowing them to serve your children and transport them safely to and from school daily, while on field trips, and during any extra curriculum activities. Father, I speak pay increases into the lives of Your bus drivers today, in Jesus' name. Everywhere a bus driver is being abused by students, Father, I silence the mouths of those children. Deliver them from strange children today in Jesus Name. I command peace to these buses now, in Jesus' name. Put Your bus drivers on display for Your glory. May prayer, in Jesus' name, break out on the school buses and may Your bus drivers be encouraged and empowered in Jesus Name.

Amen

Prayer for Assistants

I speak to every assistant in the educational arena who feels inadequate, looked over, overlooked, unimportant, and less skilled. May you rise today, in Jesus' name. I reverse every word curse spoken over you by others and even yourselves. Father, I come against the spirit of fear that would keep them from pursuing degrees to become teachers, educators, administrators, or the like if that is their desire. God has not given any assistant the spirit of fear, but a spirit of power, love, and a sound mind. They shall walk in that decree today. Father, everywhere an assistant is struggling to pass any assessments needed for licensure, we ask You give them a mind to learn, grace to study, a strategy to go back to school, take courses, and complete whatever is needed to become qualified in Jesus Name. Father, even as I pray for assistants, please assist me today in Jesus Name. I bring You my schedule today. Show me how to maximize my time and prioritize what needs to be prioritized. I have decided to seek Your kingdom first. Send help from the sanctuary to help execute this plan for me as well as every assistant connected to the academic system in Jesus Name.

Amen

Prayer for Retired Teachers

Father, I call forth Your retired teachers to come and mentor and help the younger teachers. The Titus 2 men and women who are retired, may you come forth alongside other educators in the academic system to be divine strategists, helpers, and laborers, in Jesus' name. May the same God who has placed others in the ministry, also place you in it and it shall be well in your mind, body and soul. Every retired educator will have longevity and health in their lives, even as Moses did. I speak to sick bodies now and say be healed, in Jesus' name. I speak to sick and decaying minds now and say be healed, in Jesus' name. May the grace of God cause every appointed teacher that has retired to arise again. May the peace of God cause them to work again alongside younger educators to bridge the gap for the glory of God. May they be strengthened, in Jesus' name, for the task at hand. May there be a sure reward on earth as there is in heaven for them. Father, those who need to retire because of health reasons or ill intentions for students, may they suddenly retire in Jesus Name.

Amen

Prayer for Substitutes

Father, I lift up ever substitute teacher to You. Some are retired teachers, some are supplementing income, some are doing it as a stepping stone into the educational arena, while some are doing it because it is a job that they can work at their own discretion. Father, whatever reason they substitute, You know and You see all. I ask that You bless them as only You know how. Give them wisdom, understanding, and insight when they step into any classroom as the second man to carry out the plans of the first one. Father, I pray for favor with substitutes. Father, I pray *Proverbs 3:1-4* over each substitute now in Jesus' name. Substitutes, do not forget God's law, but let your heart keep His commands; for length of days, long life and peace, they will be added to you. Do not let mercy and truth forsake you, but bind them around your neck, write them on the tablet of your heart, *And* you will find favor and high esteem in the sight of God, man, school boards, teachers, educators, parents, principals and students, in Jesus' name. You will be wise as serpents, but harmless as doves. You will speak with accuracy and instruct with precision. You will disciple with a firm yet loving hand. You are not beneath the teacher but an addition to what he or she brings to the table. *Exodus 17:12* declares, *"Moses' arms soon became so tired he could no longer hold them up. So, Aaron and Hur found a stone for him to sit on. Then they stood on each side of Moses, holding up his hands. So, his hands held steady until sunset"* (New Living Translation). For I declare today that each substitute operates as a Moses to each educator. For you hold up their arms when they get tired and God calls you blessed. You are appreciated and honored. May the Lord make every substitute's effortssuccessful; yes, may the Lord make their efforts successful, in Jesus' Name. Every wicked and diabolical substitute, I drive you out with the blood of Jesus. May you choke on the blood and never be able to carry out the evil plans and plots from the enemy over this generation again in Jesus Name. Father screen the applicants that have applied to be a substitute and only let those who meet your qualifications receive employment.

Amen

Prayer for School Resource Officers

Father I lift up every school resource officer to You, in Jesus' Name. I am praying that they have a heart to serve Your people and serve wholeheartedly at their respective places of employment. Father, I pray that they serve these children with integrity and respect. According to *1 Samuel 14:7, "So his armor bearer said to him, "Do all that is in your heart. Go then; here I am with you, according to your heart"*. Father, as school resource officer can be liken to armor bearers, I thank You that they support the vision of the principal in each school and carry out their righteous plans. Even in *1 Samuel 31:4* as Saul asked his armor bearer, to kill him with his sword, the armorbearer would not, for he was greatly afraid. So, shall it be with the school resource officers. May they carry out only righteous plans of the authorities. Father, circumcise and weed out those who have ill motives and intentions for Your children. Weed out and expose those who racially and socio-economically profile students. May the hand of you God, deal with them today in Jesus Name. Soften their hearts and may they turn to You for forgiveness and repentance. Father, I pray *Psalm 91* over their lives as they stand in the gap to protect and serve a school, a community of children, and a staff of educators and adults. Father, dispatch Your angels to watch over them now, in Jesus' name. May no hurt, harm, or danger come near them while on the job and while they are off. May they have a long, prosperous life in You, for they will carry out Your will and Your plans in the school systems, in Jesus' name.

Amen

Prayer for Secretaries and Office Support Staff

Father, I am lifting up every secretary to You in Jesus Name. Father, as they can be liken to scribes in Your Word, I ask that You place a supernatural ability and grace upon them to write and transcribe as if they were transcribing Your words. Father, bless their hands like never before, in Jesus' name. Father, bless the works of their hands. Teach their hands to war and their fingers to fight. Teach their hands to war and their fingers to type. Teach their hands to war and their fingers to write, in Jesus' Name. Father, open their eyes that they may see and open their ears that they may hear. Father, I pray that the secretaries in Your schools are godly secretaries greeting parents, greeting adults, and greeting students with the love of Jesus Christ. I pray that every secretary in the educational arena is full of love and compassion, slow to get angry and kind to all people. May they reflect Your heart and work as if they are serving unto You. Father, set Your words in their mouths today. Father, set a watch over the door of their lips and may their words be seasoned with salt. May their countenance and demeanor be changed by the power and glory of Your presence. Visit each secretary today and bless them as only You know how. Father, as You trust these secretaries with classified and important pieces of information concerning the day-to- day operation of schools, staff members, students, parents, and other adults, Father make them well aware of their importance and significance in the educational arena. Father you have given secretaries power because they have knowledge. Father you have given secretaries authority because they have knowledge. Father, let every secretary walk in the integrity and confidence that is needed for a task and job such as this. I dismantle, disallow, and destroy the secretaries in the school system that falsely pen information independently or under the leadership and instruction of others. I cancel their assignment of falsehood, in Jesus' name. Father, raise up these secretaries as teachers of Your law and confidants to your administrators and staff members. Raise their level of pay now, in Jesus' name. Increase them on every side as you increase their finances in Jesus' name.

Amen

Prayer for Cafeteria Workers and Food Service Providers

Father, I thank You for every food service provider and cafeteria worker who serves Your children and the schools. Father, I ask that You circumcise the hearts of Your people and Your school cafeteria workers today, in Jesus' name. Father, raise them up and let them know they are some of the most important individuals in the educational system. Father, let Your love engulf them like a tsunami and I break off rejection and low self-worth because of the job they perform. Father, as some students only come to school for safety and a meal, allow these workers to see how valuable and important they are as individuals and how valuable the service they provide is. Let each student be served as if the workers were serving Jesus. Father, let them cook with the love of Jesus Christ and serve with joy. Father, let Your love exude from their loins as they prepare these meals with care. May what is provided by food service workers be healthy and nourishing to the bodies of those who consume it. Father, even if meat is provided, let students prefer vegetables to eat and water to drink. May children desire a consecrated meal at school while they are seeking Your face. Father, I thank You for the lives of each food service worker now and I pray increase on every side of their lives now, in Jesus' name. Increase their finances now, in Jesus' name. I speak increase in their family and future now, in Jesus' name. Father, raise Your workers up to be great leaders and mentors even in the schools. Give them words to speak to Your children daily when they come through the line. Give them wisdom and insight like never before. Raise them up to be Your weapons of war that shatters nations and destroys kingdoms that are working in the schools that are contrary to Your will. Father, do it for Your name sake. (*Dan. 1:12, Jer. 51:20 New Life Version*)

Amen

Prayer for Custodial Staff

Father, I thank You for every custodial and janitorial employee in the educational system. Father, I thank You for their lives and their hearts to serve others. May they serve the schools, the students, and other adults as if they are serving unto You. I pray today that You blanket them with Your love and Your kindness. May they never feel less than or inadequate based on the title they carry or the job description they have. Father, thank You that You will not withhold any good thing from those that are blameless. Lord may these custodial workers be found blameless today in Jesus Name. Father, let them honor You with their bodies in the way they live, work, and eat. May they always have enough to take care of their needs. Father, for every custodial worker and janitor that desires promotion, may You grant it to them, in Jesus' name. It is You who judges, so may You decide today who will rise and not fall. May they rise, in Jesus' name. I pray Father that they are respected and honored on a daily basis in Jesus' Name. (*Psalm 84:11, 1 Cor. 6:20, Psalm 75:6-7 New Life Version*)

Amen

Prayer for Students

Father God, I stand in proxy for students around the world. Every child is a gift from You. Thank You for the gifts You have given this world. I ask now that You stretch Your hand out and touch every student everywhere right now, in the name of Jesus. Every demonic and satanic assignment that has been assigned to them, I command it to be broken now, in Jesus' mighty name. Locate any hindering spirits now and burn them up, in Jesus' mighty name.

Ezekiel 22:30-31 reads, *"So I sought for a man among them who would make a wall, and stand in the gap before Me on behalf of the land, that I should not destroy it; but I found no one. Therefore I have poured out My indignation on them; I have consumed them with the fire of My wrath; and I have recompensed their deeds on their own heads," says the Lord God"* (New King James Version).

Father, I stand in the gap on behalf of the educational system in this land that You should not destroy it. Lord, do not pour Your indignation out on us and do not let us be consumed with the fire of Your wrath. Reverse the curse that is upon this generation. Go back ten generations and remove the curse off of our babies. Father I make up the hedge and close the gap. Use me for Your glory to impact and make a change in the educational system.

Thank You, Abba Father, for being a high tower where these students can run to and find shelter and safety in You. Protect them as they leave school, daily. Protect them while they are in school, daily. Father, protect them as they are in the locker rooms changing, using the correct bathroom assigned to them by you. Protect them in their classes, in the cafeteria, and any other areas they may find themselves throughout the school day. Bless their comings and goings every day in Jesus' name. Light up their path so they can see the way You want them to travel. Anoint their heads with oil. May they honor their parents because it is right and pleases You. May they live a long, prosperous, and abundant life. Strengthen homes now, in Jesus' name, where each student is raised in the fear and admonition of You. Father, set Your words in their mouths and may they be set on fire for Your glory. Father, I pray every gift, talent, and skill You have given them will be used for Your glory. I speak *Isaiah 22:22* over each student's life now that declares the door You close, no man will be able to open, and the door You open, no man will be able to shut. Father, every emotional, psychological, physical, social, or mental issue that any student is dealing with now, I ask You to give these students strength to endure. Let every demonic and satanic attack sent to them be broken off now, in Jesus' mighty name. Raise up role models whom they can trust and confide in.

Circumcise each role model, teacher, coach, counselor, minister, or friend that these children may confide in that it will not be turned back around on them as manipulation, blackmail, or abuse in any form. I come against sexual abuse, mental abuse, psychological abuse, emotional abuse, and any other form of abuse against any student in Jesus Name. Teach each role model to love like You so the students can trust in You and the people You send in their lives. Give each student teachers after Your own heart. Every teacher who stands in opposition of Your Word and will, Father, I ask You to cut them down now, in Jesus' mighty name. Every witch that is operating in the school system I ask that they be exposed and dealt with by Your omnipotent hand. Help these students to take a stand for righteousness. Give them a quiet confidence and a courageous boldness in Jesus Christ. Father, help each student be an example in their homes and to other classmates, peers, students, and adults in their buildings, and other areas of influence. Father, do it for Your name sake. Father, I am asking the Lord of the Harvest to send forth laborers into the educational arena and harvest Your field, according to *Luke 10:2*. Abba Father, direct their steps so they can keep Your statutes according to *Psalm 119:5*. Father, according to *Matthew 15:13* every plant that has been planted in the educational system that has not been planted by You, I uproot it now in the power, authority, and name of Jesus. Let them alone be blind leaders leading the blind and they all fall into the ditch dug by Almighty God. Father, let them not use foul or abusive language. Let everything they say be good and helpful, so that their words will be an encouragement to those who hear them. Father, I command that these parents do not bring sorrow to God's Holy Spirit by the way they live. Father, I speak to their very spirits now and say get rid of all bitterness, rage, anger, harsh words, and slander, as well as all types of evil behavior. Instead, be kind to each other, tenderhearted, forgiving one another, just as God, through Christ, has forgiven them. Father, according to *2 Corinthians 5:18-20*, *"All of this is a gift from God, who brought us back to himself through Christ. And God has given us this task of reconciling people to him. For God was in Christ, reconciling the world to himself, no longer counting people's sins against them. And he gave us this wonderful message of reconciliation"* (New Living Translation). So as I am Christ's ambassador; God is making His appeal through me. I speak for Christ when I plead, "Come back to God!" For God made Christ, who never sinned, to be the offering for my sin, so that I could be made right with God through Christ. Thank you Father.

Bless every teacher. Bless every administrator. Bless every staff member. Bless every custodial worker. Help individuals respect all partakers and stakeholders in the school systems who make these academic institutions function and flow. Bless every cafeteria worker. Bless every guidance counselor. Bless every social worker and psychologist. Bless every student who sits in a classroom or comes through the educational system whether private, public, or home school. Bless the public schools. Bless the private schools. Bless the Christian and charter schools. Bless the Catholic and Muslim schools. Bless your people. May the love of Jesus Christ draw them all to You. May the love You show and the love of Your people draw them. Bless every boarding school and every military school. Bless every student, parent, and teacher that is connected to home-schools. Bless the technical schools, beauty schools, and trade schools. Bless job corps and students in the military. Bless every school of ministry and every ministry that teaches people how to serve Your people. Bless every daycare and daycare provider. Bless the children in the womb and those who are not even here yet. Bless home day care facilities so they will be operable and able to follow and maintain all guidelines that provide an orderly and safe environment for children. Bless every nanny, every grandmother, and every grandfather. Bless every aunt, uncle, big sister, or big brother who serves as caretakers of children. Bless the colleges, universities, and higher institutions of learning, in Jesus' name. Bless every organization that has been and will join the wall of prayer, crying out to You for help in the schools. I apply the blood of Jesus over the doorposts of those involved in this prayer and each child that will be affected. The blood of Jesus covers these schools in these United States of America now, in Jesus' name. Father, soak the schools across this globe in the blood of Jesus. Father, I lift up each educational system in the United States of America. I lift up every academic institution across this globe for your name sake. Rope off each school with a blood-soaked wall, where the blood of Jesus is smeared within a fifty-mile radius and giant warring angels have been dispatched to stand guard. Encamp giant warring angels around each school to protect it from the wiles of the enemy. I am girded up and have on my armor to fight.

Father, raise up Your believers to lead and excel in every arena of the educational system. Raise up believing teachers, assistants, administrators, consultants, principals, deans, professors, daycare owners, daycare workers, accountants, chancellors, specialists, coaches, administrative assistants, governmental officials, judges, resource officers, policemen, senators, congressmen and women, presidents, social workers, psychologists, case managers, and counselors. Father, as You raise them up, shake out the wicked ones. Sit them down now, in Jesus' name.

Father do great and astounding things in these schools and school systems in Jesus Name. The blind will receive their sight. The lame will walk. Lepers will be cleansed. The deaf will hear. The dead will be raised up and the poor shall have the gospel preached to them. Blessed is he, whosoever shall not be offended in the name of Jesus Christ. Let everyone in these schools be grounded in love.

Father, cover every institution in the blood of Jesus. Father, bless teachers who are abroad teaching and who are applying to teach abroad. If it is Your will, allow their paperwork to be expedited. According to Your Word in *Psalm 144:11 "Rid me, and deliver me from the hand of strange children, whose mouth speaketh vanity, and their right hand is a right hand of falsehood:"* (King James Version).

Habakkuk 1:4-5 declares, *"Therefore the law is slacked, and judgment doth never go forth: for the wicked doth compass about the righteous; therefore wrong judgment proceedeth. Behold ye among the heathen, and regard, and wonder marvelously: for I will work a work in your days, which ye will not believe, though it be told you"*

(King James Version). Father work Your work in our days. Work a work that we will not be able to comprehend or understand, nonetheless work a work on behalf of Your people.

I write the vision now in heaven on behalf of the educational system. Father, I write prayer only, in Jesus' name, back into every school. I cancel, annul, and destroy the tracking system in schools. I destroy exclusionary laws for Christian degrees in the educational arenas. Let every district and school accept degrees that are Christian based. Let Christians advance like never before in the educational system. I write textbook policies that would be inclusive of all people and all facts. Sign the law now with the pen drilling with the rich red blood of Jesus. Lord let Your chief angel deliver the law to the appropriate persons here on earth. Deliver the law, declare the degree, seal the order, in the name of Jesus. Destroy every gender law contrary to Your Word in the educational arena. Obliterate the federal laws of withholding money if states do not comply. Write policy that would make each state receive adequate funds to operate on a budget that is conducive and beneficial for all parties involved. Write in raises and bonuses for Your teachers, administrators, school personnel, and all staff. Make the educational arena the highest paid profession. Write Your policy and sign it in heaven, Jesus. I sever the head of every satanic charge that has been sent against us, the school systems, the educational arenas, and in our homes now, in Jesus' name.

Shame every proud person. Shame every person full of pride that is operating in the educational system. Put what You want to be learned back into the schools. Raise up godly textbook companies, godly consultants and trainers, raise up godly leaders, policy makers, senators, judges, and police. Father, thank You for godly resource officers and security officers in the schools. I thank You, Father, that a day will come when no officers will be needed in the schools.

Father, plead our cause, O Lord, with them that strive with us, that strive with these children. Fight against them that fight against us, that fight against these children. Take hold of shield and buckler, and stand up for mine help and stand up for these children's help. Draw out also the spear, and stop the way against them that persecute them, that persecute us: say unto our souls, we are thy salvation. Let them be confounded and put to shame that seek after our souls: let them be turned back and brought to confusion that devise our hurt. Let them be as chaff before the wind, and let the angel of the Lord chase them. Let their way be dark and slippery, and let the angel of the Lord persecute them. For without cause have they hid from us their net in a pit, which without cause they have dug for our souls. Let destruction come upon him unawares; and let his net that he hath hid catch himself: into that very destruction let him fall.

Father, I thank You that there will not be any murders and killings in the schools this year, in Jesus' mighty name. Every plan of murder that has been devised, I murder and kill you now by the power and authority of Jesus Christ. I stand against bullies and fighting in the schools now, in Jesus' mighty name. I declare that the 2017-2018 year will be a righteous year for children. Every accident that is designed to wreck school buses and modes of transportation, we wreck you now in the spirit, in Jesus' name. Every bomb that is planned or will be planned, we spoil your plan now and blow you up with the balm in Gilead now, in Jesus' name.

Open each child's mind to hear and give them the ear of the learned. God help Your children to know that You love them and not to compare themselves to what they see in the mean media world. Father, help them deal with self- esteem and body image issues. Place positive role models in their lives to help them cope and deal with the pressures of this culture and generation. Father I depress depression right now over the lives of this now and next generation in Jesus Name. May you give each child a quiet confidence and a courageous boldness in you.

Every tongue that rises up against these prayers in this book, God condemns according to *Isaiah 54:17*. Help us be bold in these days as we take a righteous stand in the schools, in the classrooms, daycares, universities, colleges, in our communities, in the streets, and in our homes. Help us not to be fearful in the faces of men as You promised to deliver us according to *Jeremiah 1:8*. Lord give the proud what they deserve as You scripted it in *Psalm 94:2*. Let Your vengeance come forth.

Father, thank You for placing on the inside of me the love of You and the desire to hate evil. Thank You for blessing the ones whom You have instructed and the ones whom You have taught, continue to teach, and will teach Your law. Thank You for giving me rest from the days of adversity until the pit is dug for the wicked. Thank You for sanctifying me with the truth of Your Word.

Father, as You have spoken in *Isaiah 60:22 "A little one shall become a thousand, and a small one a strong nation. I, the Lord, will hasten it in its time"* (King James Bible). So, Father, as I join with my brothers and sisters in the body of Christ to petition You on behalf of the children and educational system, I am asking that You make us mighty on our jobs and make us mighty in the educational arena. Make us strong and even as this may be a tiny number now, let there be great impact and influence for Your name sake. Father, let us become tens of thousands proclaiming the Gospel of Jesus Christ. Father, give Your angels charge over us to keep us in all of Your ways. Abba Father, You are so powerful and worthy that Your miracles, ways, laws, and decrees are recorded for the generations that have not even been born yet. Let this prayer affect the next ten generations. Let this prayer make it better for the next generation that shall live, if the return of Jesus Christ is delayed. Father, as it declares in *Psalm 103:20* I command the angels to carry out Your plans for the educational system.

Father, help me be a protector of children and raise them in the fear and admonition of You. Let godly parents arise and take their rightful places in their homes. Let godly parenting start first in the home. Help each parent today Father. Help each guardian today Father. You know every dilemma and every circumstance. You know every financial need that awaits each parent during each calendar year. Allow these children to have the necessary supplies and clothing they need for school.

Father, I receive the Word written in this prayer and I believe it now. Do it for Your glory. Do it for Your name sake. No man, no woman, and no person can take the credit for this, but I give You all the glory and all the honor for answering these prayers. All praise is due to You and I shall never take the credit for anything that You have done. May these prayers be mixed with the smoke of the incense, that ascend to

You, God, from the altar where the angel have poured them out. I come against retaliation, backlash and revenge now, in Jesus' mighty name for these prayers.

Your Word says that before I even finish praying, You have already answered them. I give You the glory and I give You the honor for answering these prayers. Thank You, Abba Father, for the victory, in Jesus' Name.

Amen

Prayer for Students with Disabilities

At the beginning of this school year (year thirteen), I came home one day and cried and cried because I told God I did not know how to teach and reach the special needs students. I had been given two middle school classes where the students were severely challenged. I had never taught kids that had such severe academic and behavioral challenges. I have kids in wheelchairs, several grades behind, and all these labels the world has put on them. They have what we call IEPs -*Individualized Educational Plans*- but God told me IEP means for you to *Intercept the Enemy's Plans* over their lives. I have prayed over them and have specifically prayed against the very labels that these children have. Take those documents that have been written about these children or other individuals and intercept the enemy's plans for their lives.

Father, I come against every spirit that is contrary to the ability You have given them. Disability means naught but You, God, has given Your children the ability to excel. Father, You have given them the ears of the learned, and You have given them the ability to live an abundant life. I decree that everything that is working in their lives that is contrary to what You have deemed their portion, I utterly destroy it and reverse it now, in Jesus' name. I command every learning defect be restored now, in Jesus' name.

Every neuron and brain deficiency be healed now, in Jesus' name. Every spirit of ADHD die by the fire of God now. The spirit of distraction die now and be loosed off of these students now, in Jesus' name. Every speech and language disability receive fire by the Holy Ghost now. *Exodus 4:10* declares, *"But Moses pleaded with the Lord, "O Lord, I'm not very good with words. I never have been, and I'm not now, even though You have spoken to me. I get tongue- tied, and my words get tangled." Then the Lord asked Moses, "Who makes a person's mouth? Who decides whether people speak or do not speak, hear or do not hear, see or do not see? Is it not I, the Lord? Now go! I will be with you as you speak, and I will instruct you in what to say."* (New Living Translation). Father, I pray today that is the portion of your children today. When they speak, it will be You speaking through them. Father according to *Mark 7:32-35*, your Word says, *"A deaf man with a speech impediment was brought to him, and the people begged Jesus to lay his hands on the man to heal him. Jesus led him away from the crowd so they could be alone. He put his fingers into the man's ears. Then, spitting on his own fingers, he touched the man's tongue. Looking up to heaven, he sighed and said, "**Ephphatha**," which means, "Be opened!" Instantly the man could hear perfectly, and his tongue was freed so he could speak plainly!"* (New Living Translation) I speak to every child who has a hearing problem and I speak to your ears and say be opened, in

Jesus' name. *John 5:8-9 "Jesus told him, 'Stand up, pick up your mat, and walk!'"* Instantly, the man was healed! He rolled up his sleeping mat and began walking! I speak to every student who is lame and cannot walk, and I say stand up and walk now, in Jesus' name. Every person who is in any special education class I say be healed now, in Jesus' name. Sweep through these institutions with your finger and touch. Touch your children now. Touch your people now. Jesus said in *Matthew 19:14-15* **"Let the children come to me. Don't stop them! For the Kingdom of Heaven belongs to those who are like these children."** *And He placed His hands on their heads and blessed them before He left."* (New Living Translation). Holy Spirit I am bringing these children to you. Lay your hands on their heads and heal them today in Jesus' Name. Father bless your children.

Amen

Prayer for Student Athletes

F ather, may every student athlete, male and female, first seek You, so all other things will be added unto them as 2 *Timothy* 2:5 declares. Athletes cannot win the prize unless they follow the rules. Help each athlete follow every rule required of them and, above all, every rule and expectation required from You. Allow them to seek validation and affirmation from You. Father, we come against the competitive spirit that makes them feellike they are less important and less valued if they do not win. I use a former student of *Simene' Walden*, David Amerson, #29, of the Oakland Raiders as a point of contact. Father, as You gave him the ears of the learned, he excelled in school and worked hard. As this young man practiced and worked throughout high school, at NC State, with the Washington Redskins, and now with the Oakland Raiders, may that be the portion of every athlete connected to this prayer. Every student who desires to play professional or semi-professional sports, may it be their portion according to the plan and purpose You have for them. May they always give You the glory for it is You who gives them the ability to perform. I come against injury, sickness, disease, and distress now, in Jesus' name. According to *1 Corinthians* 9:25, You said everyone who competes in the games exercises self-control in all things. May they exercise self-

117

control on a daily basis. Father, help each athlete to run and work hard to win. Father, I know with man some things are impossible, but with You all things are possible. I am praying to You Father, the God of possible. I use Blueford College in Virginia as another point of contact. Holy Spirit fall on these student athletes like never before. Visit them in a fresh way today. Give them supernatural ability to excel and out perform their peers academically, socially, mentally, and physically. May they never be prideful or take any credit for their ultimate success, for it will be Your doing and it is marvelous in Your sight. So, it shall be the portion of each student athlete today as it is in *Psalm 18:32*. Your Word says You, God, arm them with strength, and You make their ways perfect. So, shall it be the portion of every athlete today, in Jesus' name.

Amen

Prayer For Emotionally Challenged/Socially Distracted Students

Father, I speak to the spirit of every emotionally challenged and socially distracted student by the authority of Jesus the Christ of Nazareth and command their souls to line up with the Word and will of God for their lives. Every damaged emotion die now by the fire of the Holy Ghost. Every emotion that is unhealthy, we reverse you now, in Jesus' name. I call forth healthy emotions in each child and student now, in Jesus' name. I call forth healthy emotions in each student, child, adult, and parent now, in Jesus' name. I sprinkle the blood of Jesus over every unhealthy emotion and I put out the flames by the salt of God's word. I unplug every agent and every single thing that is charging against these children's lives now, in Jesus' name. I unplug every agent and everything that is charging against my life today, in Jesus' name. Every student who is socially challenged, I command his or her social skills be turned and used for God's glory. May God rise up in every student who loves to talk and communicate, to be his mouthpiece in the earth realm. Father, fill these student mouths with good things. Let everything they say be seasoned with salt and edifying and glorifying to You. Father, may their mouths be filled with Your love, Your words, and Your decrees. Father, break the influence of the world off of these children's minds now, in Jesus' name. Father, help students supernaturally control their desires to talk at the wrong time where they have become a distraction to the learning environment. Father, I release self-control into the lives of Your students now, in Jesus' name. I release long-suffering, kindness, gentleness, and patience into the lives of these young people now, in Jesus' name.

Amen

Prayer for "At-Risk Teens"

Father, in the name of Jesus Christ of Nazareth, I apply the blood of Jesus over the lives of every child and every student who has made, will make, and continues to make bad decisions. Father, I pray *Ephesians 6:1* over the lives of Your children now. I speak that these students will honor their fathers and mothers. I pray that these children will be raised in the fear and admonition of You. Father, if these children do not have good examples in their home, place people in their lives that will be good examples to mentor, mold, and teach them, in Jesus' name. Father, let the parents not provoke their children to anger by the way they treat them. Every teen that has been labeled as "at-risk" I reverse the word curse that has been spoken and written over their lives now, in Jesus' name. I erase the writings that are on the wall of their lives and in their subconscious minds. I beat down every thought and every imagination that exalts itself above the knowledge of who You have called them to be. Father, help them take captive those thoughts today, in Jesus' name. I abolish and end the cycle of prison in their lives and in their generation. I break down generational curses of incarceration in jails, prisons, and juvenile facilities. Father, rewrite the writings on the hearts of Your children and students. I chase away the spirits that are causing them to act out in school and to act out in the home.

Every label that has been placed on these children that does not align with Your will and Word for their lives, I cancel it and destroy it now, in Jesus' name. Father, according to *Psalm 59:1-2*, rescue Your children from their enemies and protect them from those who want to destroy them. Father, everyone and everything that is rising against this generation and these children, do not kill them because they will soon forget Your lessons, but stagger them with Your power and bring them to their knees. Father, let those who seek after the souls of these children be ashamed, confounded, and made to turn back in shame and disgrace. Father, make every person that has spoken against the lives of these students and children, swallow their own bitter and nasty words. Father, break the teeth of those who speak evil words and create negative stereotypes and comments about Your chosen people. Every adolescent, teen, young adult, adult, and mature adult who has been labeled as "at-risk", Father, I declare that today they have become "at-risk" to the kingdom of darkness and it's plan over their lives. Redirect their steps so that their steps are now ordered by You. Let Your word be a lamp unto their feet and a light unto their path according to *Psalm 119:105*. Father, I thank You that Your people are now "at-risk" to the enemy. I thank You that You have raised these students up to be "at-risk" to the enemy. Father, I thank You that their lives are a hazard to the enemy. They will take risks sharing the gospel of Jesus Christ in their schools, on their buses, with their teachers, and with their classmates and peers. Father, thank You that these students will take risks at schools to answer questions, read aloud, participate in class, and do their classwork and homework. Father, let these students take a risk to try out for sports and participate in school activities without intimidation or fear. Father, give these students a righteous boldness to take a risk to serve You and share the gospel of Jesus Christ without compromise. Do it for your Name Sake. (Psalm 59:1- 2 New Life Version)

Amen

Prayer for Academically Gifted Students

Father, I thank You for every student who excels academically. May they never grow arrogant and full of pride. May they always recognize and depend on You for their smarts, brains, and intellect. May they never be wise in their own eyes, but fear You. Help these children depart and run away from evil. Father, allow their intellect to be used for Your glory. Every gift and talent that You have given them, may it be used to uplift and build the kingdom of God. May these children impact and influence their generation in a positive and profound way. May they make discoveries that have been hidden for centuries and may they create new ways to get wealth and be kingdom financiers. May these students have balance within their lives and enjoy being a child without being submerged into work. Father, I lift up their parents to You now. May they not pressure their child to excel or out-perform others to the point it becomes a burden and extremely overwhelming. May parents not live through their child vicariously and put unreasonable and unfair demands on their child. I break anxiety and stress off of these children now, in Jesus' name. May the competitive spirit be broken off of these children now, in Jesus' name. Depression, inadequacy, and low self-esteem will not be their portion. Success, overflow, and abundance of grace, peace, prosperity, and joy in Jesus Name shall be their portion.

Amen

Prayer Against Sexual Sins in The Educational System

Father, I stand on behalf of these children, these students, and these adults. Lord, do not pour Your indignation out on us and do not let us be consumed by the fire of Your wrath. Reverse the curse that is upon this generation. Go back ten generations and remove the curse off of our babies. Father, I break the generational curse of sexual sins of rape, incest, and molestation from everyone who is connected to these prayers today, tomorrow, and forever more. Use me for Your glory to impact and make a change in the educational system. Father, your Word said in *Proverbs 18:10* *"The name of the Lord is a strong tower; the righteous runneth into it and is safe"* (English Standard Version). Father, may Your people, may the victim and the victimizer, run into the strong tower today. May some accidently run and may some intentionally run into the strong tower today. Father, I pray *2 Corinthians 1:3-5 today. "All praise to God, the Father of our Lord Jesus Christ. God is our merciful Father and the source of all comfort. He comforts us in all our troubles so that we can comfort others. When they are troubled, we will be able to give them the same comfort God has given us. For the more we suffer for Christ, the more God will shower us with his comfort through Christ. Even when we are weighed down with troubles, it is for your comfort and salvation! For when we ourselves are comforted, we will certainly comfort you. Then you can patiently endure the same things we suffer. We are confident that as you share in our sufferings, you will also share in the comfort God gives us"* (New Living Translation). Father, in the name of Jesus, I ask that You set these children, these students, and these educators who have been raped or molested free, in Jesus' name. Father, in the name of Jesus, I ask You to free them from tormenting spirits. Father, set them free from spirits of molestation, spirits of rape, and spirits of murder, in the name of Jesus. I torment every tormenting spirit now in Jesus' name. I curse the curse now, in Jesus' name. I kill the spirit of killing now in Jesus' name. I snuff you out today with burning sulfur in Jesus' name. I molest every spirit of molestation with the fire of the Holy Ghost and the blood of Jesus. I rape the spirit of rape now in Jesus Name. I sodomize the spirit of sodomy with the fire of the Holy Ghost. Save Lord. Save Your people today, Lord. Save the rapist today. Send someone to minister the love of Jesus to them now in Jesus Name. Father, save the pedarest today. Save the pedophile and those who practices bestiality this morning. Save the adulterer and fornicator this morning, in Jesus' name. Save Lord. I am crying out for souls so the perversion and the sin can stop. We are calling for souls this morning. Save the sexually confused in Jesus Name. Save Lord. Save the predator. Save the liar and save the abuser today in Jesus Name. Save them now, Jesus. They are hurting and need You and that is why they keep hurting others and themselves, but save them from themselves. Save the molester who is working in the schools with children. Save the coach who has a history of molesting little boys on the team. Save the female educator who sleeps with little boys because she never grew out of the little girl stage after she was sexually violated. Save Your people today Lord. Save Lord.

Father, I ask that you heal the victim and victimizer from all bound and blocked memory recall that has affected them because of molestation. Deliver them from any and all spiritual bondage that came through it, in Jesus' name. Father, send someone in their lives that they can confess their sins to and receive the necessary treatment and healing, in Jesus' name. For Your words declare in *James 5:16, "Confess your sins to each other and pray for each other so that you may be healed"* (New International Version). The earnest prayer of a righteous person has great power and produces wonderful results. Elijah was as human as I am, and yet when he prayed earnestly that no rain would fall, none fell for three and a half years! Then, when he prayed again, the sky sent down rain and the earth began to yield its crops.

Father today I stand as Your oracle and I say that sexual sins in the schools shall stop today, in Jesus' name. For three years, sexual sins will cease in the educational arena and in three years those who have not repented and changed their ways, shall be exposed and utterly destroyed, in Jesus' name. May many souls be saved during this three-year time span. I declare it and I stand firmly on this Word today. It is so. It is established in heaven so it now becomes established on this earth and in these United States of America educational system. Father, I glorify You for hearing my prayers, healing Your people, healing this educational system, healing Your students, and healing Your educators, in Jesus' name. For when I step into my sphere of influence today, miracles, signs, and wonders shall follow me and I will glorify you as my God. May I always represent you well and never shame your name. I thank you in advance for answering these prayers in Jesus Name.

Amen

Prayer for Deliverance from Trouble

Every trouble that has troubled me, troubled a child, or a student, has just been troubled by the Holy Ghost, in Jesus' name. Everything that is currently troubling us, may the trouble of the Holy Ghost trouble it now in Jesus' name. I am part of this generation who seeks the face of God and no devil in hell can stop that. Everything that comes to hinder me, I hinder and trap it by the power and authority of God. Every stop sign and road-block that has been placed in my life, I call the demolition crew of Jesus Christ to demolish it. Every construction site that has been built and is being built around my life, has just been run over and brought low, in Jesus' name. Thank you Jesus for destroying it in Jesus' name. I call forth the implosion of the Holy Ghost to implode on the enemy that is harassing my life. The Lord will cause any demonic foundation that has been built in my life to crumple and catch fire today. Every structure that has been built outside of the will of God, will collapse now by the implosion of Jesus Christ. I take the crane of Jesus and lift every heavy burden, every piece of demonic and satanic material that has been built around my life and my family's life, and I transport them to the pits of hell now, in Jesus' name. May the spiritual bulldozer of Jesus chase down every demonic infrastructure that is operating in my life. Lord, I want to be a child of You and I want to live a life that is pleasing in Your eyes. Father, I am not a child that has been left behind. Father, send the angels of war to release me from captivity now, in Jesus' name. May the angels that You have assigned to me release them now, in Jesus' name. I am not left behind in the natural and I am not a child left behind in the spirit. I receive speed now to run past those who do not like me, hate on me, unfriend me, betray me, and lie on me. May my feet become like feet of deer that can run fast and pass them. I pull down every high place that is operating in my life and I have victory today, in Jesus' name.

Amen

Prayer For Educational Institutions And Organizations

Please keep these places lifted to the Lord in your daily prayers. Ask God to cover these places in the blood of Jesus. Ask God to protect and pour love on each individual who attends any of these schools, past or present. Ask God to protect and love on the individuals who work in these schools, past or present. Ask the Lord to protect and love on the adults who work in these schools, attend these churches, or partake in any of these businesses at any level. Ask God to blanket them with His grace, love, peace, prosperity, and joy, in Jesus' name.

Buck Lodge Middle School, Adelphi, Maryland

Sugar Creek Charter School, Charlotte, North Carolina

Sugar Creek High School, Charlotte, North Carolina

Douglas Byrd Middle, Fayetteville, North Carolina

Guilford Prep Academy, Greensboro, North Carolina

Jackson Middle School, Greensboro, North Carolina

Enfield Middle School, Enfield, North Carolina

Northridge Middle School, Charlotte, North Carolina

Washington Montessori, Greensboro, North Carolina

Guilford County Schools, North Carolina

Prince George's County Schools, Maryland

Northampton County Schools, North Carolina

Conway Middle Schools, Conway, North Carolina

Northampton County Schools, Jackson, North Carolina

Hertford County Schools, North Carolina

Bertie County Schools, North Carolina

Halifax County Schools, North Carolina

Nash-Rocky Mount Schools, North Carolina

Pitt County Schools, North Carolina

Pender County, North Carolina

Willis Hare Elementary School, Pendleton, North Carolina

KIPP Gaston, Gaston, North Carolina

Cabarrus County Schools, Concord, North Carolina

Currituck County Schools, North Carolina

Pasquotank County Schools, North Carolina

Dare County Schools, North Carolina

Charlotte Mecklenburg Schools, Charlotte, North Carolina

West Mecklenburg High School, Charlotte, North Carolina

Easter Seals School, Upland, California

Emilie Ritchen Middle School, California

Roanoke Rapids Graded School, Roanoke Rapids, North Carolina

Miller Motte College Greenville Campus, Greenville, North Carolina

Carrollton High School, Georgia Carrollton City Schools, Georgia

District of Columbia Public Schools, Washington, DC

Lyseth Elementary School, Portland, Maine

Anne Arundel Schools, Maryland

Montgomery County Schools, Maryland

Howard County Schools, Maryland

Baltimore City Schools, Maryland

Baltimore County Schools, Maryland

Ecorse High School, Ecorse, Michigan

Detroit Public Schools, Michigan

Maine Public Schools, Maine

Wood Stream Academy, Bowie, Maryland

Samuel P. Massie, Forestville, Maryland

Eastside High School, Greenville, South Carolina

Greer Middle College, Greenville, South Carolina

Suitland High School, Suitland, Maryland

Francis Scott Key Elementary School, District Heights, Maryland

Cheltenham High School, Wyncote, Pennsylvania

Cheltenham School District, Elkins Park, Pennsylvania

School District of Philadelphia, Philadelphia, Pennsylvania

Philadelphia Juvenile Justice Center, Philadelphia, Pennsylvania

Philadelphia Learning Academy North, Philadelphia, Pennsylvania

Philadelphia Learning Academy South, Philadelphia, Pennsylvania

Crossroads Accelerated Academy, Philadelphia, Pennsylvania

Sandy Grove Middle School, Lumber Bridge, North Carolina

Hoke County Schools, North Carolina

Union County, Monroe, Wadesboro, North Carolina

Anson County Schools, Anson, North Carolina

Durham County Schools, Durham, North Carolina

Wake County Public Schools, Cary, North Carolina

Mississippi Department of Education, Jackson, Mississippi

Teach for America, Nationwide

Department of Family & Children Services, Georgia

Carolina Behavioral Developmental Hospital, Charlotte, North Carolina

North Carolina Division of Services for the Blind, North Carolina

Bluefield College, Bluefield, Virginia

Fayetteville State University, Fayetteville, North Carolina

North Carolina A&T University, Greensboro, North Carolina

Bowie State University, Bowie, Maryland

Halifax Community College, Weldon, North Carolina

Roanoke Chowan Community College, Ahoskie, North Carolina

Grand Canyon University, Phoenix, Arizona

University of Maryland College Park, College Park, Maryland

Department of Education, District of Columbia

Secretary of Education, District of Columbia

United States Supreme Court, District of Columbia

Temple of Praise International Church members, Beltsville, Maryland

University City Church members, Huntersville, North Carolina

New Light Missionary Baptist Church members, Greensboro, North Carolina

CoverGirlsNC, Charlotte, North Carolina

Empowering the Youth, Charlotte, North Carolina

Step Up to Leadership Mentoring Program, Gastonia, North Carolina

DLeeInspires, Atlanta, Georgia

Cleveland Moms in Prayer, Cleveland, Ohio

The Movement Process with Sean Wyman, Wakulla Springs, Florida

Changing Minds Online, Dr. Aikyna Finch and Vanessa Canteberry

A Million Heartbreaks, Lithonia, Georgia

Authors in Business

Amen

Testimonials

Precious Woman of God I'm so grateful for the live video Teacher Student-prayer call in the morning. I was disappointed because my cell carrier no longer allows free calling to prayer lines. I had connected with three, which I'm no longer able to pray with. When I found your live prayer call it was a blessing and a release. It provides an opportunity for me to unite in prayer with like-minded people who are providing education, training, support and services to youth. It released me to connect in the spirit realm with others so the strength of our prayers, not just my prayer, can make earth resemble God's mandate from Heaven. I'm not a teacher. I'm a counselor. Your obedience to God in bringing this prayer wheel into the earth will be the means that someone's child will be set free, delivered, saved, empowered, launched into their purpose. You are a conduit for the voice of God and the will of God to impact education systems. You have afforded me the blessed privilege of putting prayer power to work early when I rise. Thank you. Remain fiercely victorious, my Sister-friend.

-Laurae, Charlotte, North Carolina

Your life has transformed right in front of my eyes. You are a mighty Prayer Warrior. Your life has caused me to want more of God and brought my faith to a new higher level. You are a blessing to me in so many ways. I love you sis. ☺

-Kimberly, Suitland, Maryland

When I say Ms. Walden sent up a powerful, fiery, Holy Ghost prayer this morning. Girl you were ON IT! Thank you, God!!! Sharing this one...the WORLD needs to hear it!!

- Denise, Trenton, North Carolina

I am so blessed by all of your prayers. Never stop praying for us. God bless you. Love you so much.

- Iva, Charlotte, North Carolina

Coming Soon: Standing On His Words:

Student Edition
Volume 1

DAY 1

Psalm 25:7 Do not remember the sins of my youth and my rebellious ways; according to your love remember me, for You, Lord, are good. (NIV)

According to research, the most important parts of your brain are not completely developed or grown until the age of twenty-five. If you have made mistakes and done things on purpose, some of that was because you did not know any better. God loves you so much and He wants you to serve Him and be His child. Ask for forgiveness of your sins and do not make the same mistakes again. Ask the Lord to forgive you of your rebellion, stubborn and mean ways, and God will.

DAY 2

Psalm 25:5 Guide me in Your truth and teach me, for You are God my Savior, and my hope is in You all day long. (NIV)

There are times when lying and not telling the truth seems to keep you out of trouble. It may keep you out of

141

trouble from people, parents, or teachers, but God sees everything. Ask God to help you not lie even when you feel pressure and even when you feel like you will get in trouble for telling the truth. The truth is better than a lie regardless of what people tell you. God's Word says it is better to tell the truth so that is what you should believe. Ask God to be your Lord and Savior and hope in Him all day. No matter what is going on around you, no matter what your friends, classmates, neighbors, cousins, or enemies are doing, always hope in God.

DAY 3

Jeremiah 1:8 Do not be afraid of them, for I am with you and will rescue you, declares the Lord. (NIV)

As a child or student, people can sometimes frighten or scare you. Seek God above all else. Do not be afraid of anyone who wants to cause you harm or try to get you into trouble. God will always be with you. Pray to Him and ask Him to help you. Do not be afraid to speak truth and tell the truth because God will deliver you from those same people who do not want you to share it.

DAY 4

Ephesians 6:1-3 Children, obey your parents in the Lord, for this is right. Honor your father and mother—which is the first commandment with a promise— so that it may go well with you and that you may enjoy long life on the earth. (NKJV)

Honor your parents because it brings God great joy when you listen to your parents. God has given your parents a huge responsibility to watch over you and raise you up. Never retaliate or disrespect your parents. Even if they do not raise or love you like you desire, need, or want, God is always there. Pray and ask Him to send those into your life who will love and take care of you if you have a parent who is not. God will handle your parents and any adult in your life. Learn to honor your parents at all time.

Resource List

Psalm 7:11 (King James Version) God judgeth the righteous, and God is angry with the wicked every day.

Psalm 94:22 (King James Version) But the Lord is my defense; and my God is the rock of my refuge.

Psalm 144:11 (King James Version) Rid me, and deliver me from the hand of strange children, whose mouth speaketh vanity, and their right hand is a right hand of falsehood.

Psalm 119:132-136 (King James Version) Look thou upon me, and be merciful unto me, as thou usest to do unto those that love thy name. Order my steps in thy word: and let not any iniquity have dominion over me. Deliver me from the oppression of man: so will I keep thy precepts. Make thy face to shine upon thy servant; and teach me thy statutes. Rivers of waters run down mine eyes, because they keep not thy law.

Amos 5:15 (King James Version) Hate the evil, love the good, and establish judgment in the gate: it may be that the Lord God of hosts will be gracious unto the remnant of Joseph.

Habakkuk 1:4-5 (King James Version) Therefore the law is slacked, and judgment doth never go forth: for the wicked doth compass about the righteous; therefore wrong judgment proceedeth. Behold ye among the heathen, and regard, and wonder marvelously: for I will work a work in your days, which ye will not believe, though it be told you.

Matthew 11:5-6 (King James Version) The blind receive their sight, and the lame walk, the lepers are cleansed, and the deaf hear, the dead are raised up, and the poor have the gospel preached to them. And blessed is he, whosoever shall not be offended in me.

Revelation 5:12... (King James Version) Worthy is the Lamb who was slain to receive power, and riches, and wisdom, and strength and honor, and glory, and blessing.

Revelation 6:15-17 (King James Version) And the kings of the earth, and the great men, and the rich men, and the chief captains, and the mighty men, and every bondman, and every free man, hid themselves in the dens and in the rocks of the mountains; And said to the mountains and rocks, Fall on us, and hide us from the face of him that sitteth on the throne, and from the wrath of the Lamb: For the great day of his wrath is come; and who shall be able to stand?

Revelation 12:6 (King James Version) And the woman fled into the wilderness, where she hath a place prepared of

God, that they should feed her there a thousand two hundred and threescore days.

Exodus 4:10-11 (New Living Translation) But Moses pleaded with the Lord, "O Lord, I'm not very good with words. I never have been, and I'm not now, even though You have spoken to me. I get tongue-tied, and my words get tangled." Then the Lord asked Moses, "Who makes a person's mouth? Who decides whether people speak or do not speak, hear or do not hear, see or do not see? Is it not I, the Lord? Now go! I will be with you as you speak, and I will instruct you in what to say.

Exodus 17:12 (New Living Translation) Moses' arms soon became so tired he could no longer hold them up. So, Aaron and Hur found a stone for him to sit on. Then they stood on each side of Moses, holding up his hands. So, his hands held steady until sunset.

Exodus 22:18 (King James Version) Thou shalt not suffer a witch to live.

Numbers 6:24-26 (New Living Translation) May the LORD bless you and protect you. May the LORD smile on you and be gracious to you. May the LORD show you his favor and give you his peace.

Deuteronomy 34:7 (English Standard Version) Moses was 120 years old when he died. His eye was undimmed, and his vigor unabated.

1 Samuel 31:4 (New Life Version) Then Saul said to the one who carried his battle-clothes, "Take your sword and cut through me with it. Or these men who have not gone through our religious act will come and kill me with the sword and make fun of me." But the one who carried his battle-clothes would not do it, for he was filled with fear. So Saul took his sword and fell on it.

2 Samuel 7:28-29 (New Living Translation) For You are God, O Sovereign Lord. Your words are truth, and You have promised these good things to Your servant. And now, may it please You to bless the house of Your servant, so that it may continue forever before You. For You have spoken, and when You grant a blessing to Your servant, O Sovereign Lord, it is an eternal blessing!

2 Chronicles 7:14 (English Standard Version)…if My people who are called by My name humble themselves and pray and seek My face and turn from their wicked ways, I will hear from heaven and will forgive their sins and heal their land.

Psalm 18:20 (New Living Translation) The Lord rewarded me for doing right; he restored me because of my innocence.

Psalm 18:29 (New Living Translation) In your strength I can crush an army; with my God I can scale any wall.

Psalm 18:30 (New Living Translation) God's way is perfect. All the Lord's promises prove true. He is a shield for all who look to him for protection.

Psalm 18:32 (New Life Version) It is God Who covers me with strength and makes my way perfect.

Psalm 18:33 (New Living Translation) He makes me as surefooted as a deer, enabling me to stand on mountain heights.

Psalm 19:14 (New International Version) May these words of my mouth and this meditation of my heart be pleasing in your sight, Lord, my Rock and my Redeemer.

Psalm 20:1-2 (New International Version) May the Lord answer you when you are in distress; may the name of the God of Jacob protect you. May he send you help from the sanctuary and grant you support from Zion.

Psalm 20:6 (New Living Translation) Now I know that the Lord rescues his anointed king. He will answer him from his holy heaven and rescue him by his great power.

Psalm 23:1-3 (New International Version) The Lord is my shepherd, I lack nothing. He makes me lie down in green pastures, he leads me beside quiet waters, he refreshes my soul. He guides me along the right paths for his name's sake.

Psalm 24:6 (King James Version) This *is* Jacob, the generation of those who seek Him, who seek Your face. *Selah*

Psalm 25:5 (New International Version) Guide me in your truth and teach me, for you are God my Savior, and my hope is in you all day long.

Psalm 25:7 (New International Version) Do not remember the sins of my youth and my rebellious ways; according to your love remember me, for you, Lord, are good.

Psalm 51:1-2 (King James Version) Have mercy upon me, O God, According to Your loving kindness; According to the multitude of Your tender mercies, Blot out my transgressions. Wash me thoroughly from my iniquity, And cleanse me from my sin.

Psalm 59:1-2 (New Life Version) O my God, take me away from those who hate me. Put me up high above those who rise up against me. Take me away from those who do wrong. And save me from those who kill.

Psalm 75:6-7 (New Life Version) For honor does not come from the east or the west or from the desert. But God is the One Who decides. He puts down one and brings respect to another.

Psalm 84:11 (New Life Version) For the Lord God is a sun and a safe- covering. The Lord gives favor and honor. He holds back nothing good from those who walk in the way that is right.

Psalm 90:17 (New International Version) May the favor of the Lord our God rest on us; establish the work of our hands for us—yes, establish the work of our hands.

Psalm 91 (New Living Translation) Those who live in the shelter of the Most High will find rest in the shadow of the Almighty. This I declare about the Lord. He alone is my refuge, my place of safety; He is my God, and I trust Him. For He will rescue you from every trap and protect you from deadly disease. He will cover you with His feathers. He will shelter you with His wings. His faithful promises are your armor and protection. Do not be afraid of the terrors of the night, nor the arrow that flies in the day. Do not dread the disease that stalks in darkness, nor the disaster that strikes at midday. Though a thousand fall at your side, though ten thousand are dying around you, these evils will not touch you. Just open your eyes, and see how the wicked are punished. If you make the Lord your refuge, if you make the Most High your shelter, no evil will conquer you; no plague will come near your home. For He will order his angels to protect you wherever you go. They will hold you up with their hands so you won't even hurt your foot on a stone. You will trample upon lions and cobras; you will crush fierce lions and serpents under your feet! The Lord says, "I will rescue those who love Me. I will protect those who trust in My name. When they call on Me, I will answer; I will be with them in trouble. I will rescue and honor them. I will reward them with a long life and give them My salvation.

Psalm 94:2 (King James Version) Lift up thyself, thou judge of the earth: render a reward to the proud.

Psalm 102:28 (New Living Translation) The children of your people will live in security. Their children's children will thrive in your presence.

Psalm 103:12 (New Living Translation) He has removed our sins as far from us as the east is from the west.

Psalm 103:20 (New Life Version) Praise the Lord, you powerful angels of His who do what He says, obeying His voice as He speaks!

Psalm 119:5 (New Life Version) O, that my ways may be always in keeping with Your Law!

Psalm 119:12-13 (New Living Translation) I praise you, O Lord; teach me your decrees. I have recited aloud all the regulations you have given us.

Psalm 119:133 (New Living Translation) Guide my steps by your word, so I will not be overcome by evil. Ransom me from the oppression of evil people; then I can obey your commandments.

Psalm 119:105 (New Life Version) Your Word is a lamp to my feet and a light to my path.

Psalm 119:126 (New International Version) It is time for you to act, Lord; your law is being broken.

Psalm 141:2-3 (New Living Translation) Accept my prayer as incense offered to you, and my upraised hands as an evening offering. Take control of what I say, O Lord, and guard my lips.

Proverbs 3:1-4 (New Living Translation) My child, never forget the things I have taught you. Store my commands in your heart. If you do this, you will live many years, and your life will be satisfying. Never let loyalty and kindness leave you! Tie them around your neck as a reminder. Write them deep within your heart. Then you will find favor with both God and people, and you will earn a good reputation.

Proverbs 8:6 (New Living Translation) Listen to me! For I have important things to tell you. Everything I say is right.

Proverbs 13:4 (New Living Translation) Lazy people want much but get little, but those who work hard will prosper.

Proverbs 12:15 (New International Version) The way of fools seems right to them, but the wise listen to advice.

Proverbs 22:6 (New Living Translation) Direct your children onto the right path, and when they are older, they will not leave it.

Proverbs 22:17 (New Living Translation) Listen to the words of the wise; apply your heart to my instruction.

Proverbs 24:1 (King James Version) Be not thou envious against evil men, neither desire to be with them.

Proverbs 29:8 (New Living Translation) Mockers can get a whole town agitated, but the wise will calm anger.

Proverbs 30:10 (New International Version) Do not slander a servant to their master, or they will curse you, and you will pay for it.

Proverbs 31:26 (New International Version) She speaks with wisdom, and faithful instruction is on her tongue.

Ecclesiastes 7:5 (New International Version) It is better to heed the rebuke of a wise person than to listen to the song of fools.

Ecclesiastes 7:21-22 (New International Version) Do not pay attention to every word people say, or you may hear your servant cursing you—for you know in your heart that many times you yourself have cursed others.

Ecclesiastes 10:20 (New International Version) Do not revile the king even in your thoughts, or curse the rich in your bedroom, because a bird in the sky may carry your words, and a bird on the wing may report what you say.

Isaiah 22:22 (New Life Translation) Then I will put on his shoulder the rule of the family of David. What he opens, no one will shut. What he shuts, no one will open.

Isaiah 54:17 (King James Version) No weapon that is formed against thee shall prosper; and every tongue that shall rise against thee in judgment thou shalt condemn. This is the heritage of the servants of the Lord, and their righteousness is of me, saith the Lord.

Jeremiah 1:1-11 (King James Version) The words of Jeremiah the son of Hilkiah, of the priests who *were* in Anathoth in the land of Benjamin, to whom the word of the Lord came in the days of Josiah the son of Amon, king of Judah, in the thirteenth year of his reign. It came also in the days of Jehoiakim the son of Josiah, king of Judah, until the end of the eleventh year of Zedekiah the son of Josiah, king of Judah, until the carrying away of Jerusalem captive in the fifth month. Then the word of the Lord came to me, saying: "Before I formed you in the womb I knew you; Before you were born I sanctified you; I ordained you a prophet to the nations." Then said I: "Ah, Lord God! Behold, I cannot speak, for I *am* a youth." But the Lord said to me: "Do not say, 'I *am* a youth,' For you shall go to all to whom I send you, And whatever I command you, you shall speak. Do not be afraid of their faces, For I *am* with you to deliver you," says the Lord. Then the Lord put forth His hand and touched my mouth, and the Lord said to me: "Behold, I have put My words in your mouth. See, I have this day set you over the nations and over the kingdoms, To root out and to pull down, To destroy and to throw down, To build and to plant." Moreover the word of the Lord came to me, saying, "Jeremiah, what do you see?" And I said, "I see a branch of an almond tree." Then the Lord said to me, "You have seen well, for I am ready to perform My word." And the word of the Lord came to me the second time, saying, "What do you see?" And I said, "I see a boiling pot, and it is facing away from the north."

Then the Lord said to me: "Out of the north calamity shall break forth On all the inhabitants of the land. For behold, I am calling All the families of the kingdoms of the north," says the Lord; "They shall come and each one set his throne At the entrance of the gates of Jerusalem, Against all its walls all around, And against all the cities of Judah. I will utter My judgments Against them concerning all their wickedness, Because they have forsaken Me, Burned incense to other gods, And worshiped the works of their own hands. "Therefore prepare yourself and arise, And speak to them all that I command you. Do not be dismayed before their faces, Lest I dismay you before them. For behold, I have made you this day A fortified city and an iron pillar, And bronze walls against the whole land— Against the kings of Judah, Against its princes, Against its priests, And against the people of the land. They will fight against you, But they shall not prevail against you. For I *am* with you," says the Lord, "to deliver you.

Jeremiah 1:8 (King James Version) Be not afraid of their faces: for I am with thee to deliver thee, saith the Lord.

Jeremiah 1:8 (New International Version) Do not be afraid of them, for I am with you and will rescue you, declares the Lord.

Jeremiah 3:14 (King James Version) "Return, O backsliding children," says the Lord; "for I am married to you. I will take you, one from a city and two from a family, and I will bring you to Zion."

Jeremiah 20:9 (New Living Translation) But if I say I'll never mention the Lord or speak in his name, his word burns in my heart like a fire. It's like a fire in my bones! I am worn out trying to hold it in! I can't do it!

Jeremiah 51:20 (New Life Version) He says, "You are My battle-ax which I use in war. With you I destroy countries. With you I destroy nations."

Daniel 1:12 (New Life Version)…Give us only vegetables to eat and water to drink.

Ezekiel 11:1-25 (New Life Version) The Spirit lifted me up and brought me to the east gate of the Lord's house which faces eastward. There I saw twenty-five men at the door of the gate. Among them I saw Jaazaniah the son of Azzur, and Pelatiah the son of Benaiah, leaders of the people.

Habakkuk 2:2 (King James Version) Then the Lord answered me and said: "Write the vision and make *it* plain on tablets, That he may run who reads it.

Zechariah 9:12 (New International Version) Return to your fortress, you prisoners of hope; even now I announce that I will restore twice as much to you.

Matthew 11:5 (New Life Version) The blind are made to see. Those who could not walk are walking. Those who have had bad skin diseases are healed. Those who could not hear are hearing. The dead are raised up to life and the Good News is preached to poor people.

Matthew 15:13 (New Life Version) He said, "Every plant that My Father in heaven did not plant will be pulled up by the roots."

Matthew 19:14 (New King James Version) Let the little children come to Me, and do not forbid them; for of such is the kingdom of heaven.

Luke 2:52 (New International Version) And Jesus grew in wisdom and stature, and in favor with God and man.

Luke 10:2 (New Life Translation) Jesus said to them, "There is much grain ready to gather. But the workmen are few. Pray then to the Lord Who is the Owner of the grainfields that He will send workmen to gather His grain.

Romans 10:9... (New King James Version) if you confess with your mouth that Jesus is Lord and believe in your heart that God raised him from the dead, you will be saved.

Romans 12:6-7 (New Living Translation) In his grace, God has given us different gifts for doing certain things well. So if God has given you the ability to prophesy, speak out with as much faith as God has given you. If your gift is serving others, serve them well. If you are a teacher, teach well.

Romans 13:1 (New Life Version) Every person must obey the leaders of the land. There is no power given but from God, and all leaders are allowed by God.

Romans 13:1-5 (New Living Translation) Everyone must submit to governing authorities. For all authority comes from God, and those in positions of authority have been placed there by God. So anyone who rebels against authority is rebelling against what God has instituted, and they will be punished. For the authorities do not strike fear in people who are doing right, but in those who are doing wrong. Would you like to live without fear of the authorities? Do what is right, and they will honor you. The authorities are God's servants, sent for your good. But if you are doing wrong, of course you should be afraid, for they have the power to punish you. They are God's servants, sent for the very purpose of punishing those who do what is wrong. So you must submit to them, not only to avoid punishment, but also to keep a clear conscience.

1 Corinthians 6:20 (New Life Version) God bought you with a great price. So honor God with your body. You belong to Him.

1 Corinthians 9:25 (New Life Version) Everyone who runs in a race does many things so his body will be strong. He does it to get a crown that will soon be worth nothing, but we work for a crown that will last forever.

Galatians 6:4-5 (New Living Translation) Pay careful attention to your own work, for then you will get the satisfaction of a job well done, and you won't need to compare yourself to anyone else. For we are each responsible for our own work.

Ephesians 5:1-2 (New Living Translation) Imitate, God, therefore, in everything you do, because you are his dear children. Live a life filled with love, following the example of Christ.

Ephesians 6:1 (New Life Version) Children, as Christians, obey your parents. This is the right thing to do.

Ephesians 6:1-3 (New International Version) Children, obey your parents in the Lord, for this is right. "Honor your father and mother"—which is the first commandment with a promise— "so that it may go well with you and that you may enjoy long life on the earth."

Ephesians 6:13-18 (New International Version) Therefore, put on the full armor of God, so that when the day of evil comes, you may be able to stand your ground, and after you have done everything, to stand. Stand firm then, with the belt of truth buckled around your waist, with the breastplate of righteousness in place, and with your feet fitted with the readiness that comes from the gospel of peace. In addition to all this, take up the shield of faith, with which you can extinguish all the flaming arrows of the evil one. Take the helmet of salvation and the sword of the Spirit, which is the word of God. And pray in the Spirit on all occasions with all kinds of prayers and requests. With this in mind, be alert and always keep on praying for all the Lord's people.

Philippians 1:3 (New Living Translation) Every time I think of you, I give thanks to my God.

Philippians 4:6-7 (New King James Version) Be anxious for nothing, but in everything by prayer and supplication, with thanksgiving, let your requests be made known to God; and the peace of God, which surpasses all understanding, will guard your hearts and minds through Christ Jesus.

Hebrews 13:8 (New International Version) Jesus Christ is the same yesterday and today and forever.

2 Timothy 2:5 (New Life Version) Anyone who runs in a race must follow the rules to get the crown.

Genesis 9:7 (New Living Translation) Now be fruitful and multiply, and repopulate the earth.

Psalm 24:1-5 (New King James Version) The earth is the Lord's, and all its fullness, The world and those who dwell therein. For He has founded it upon the seas, And established it upon the waters. Who may ascend into the hill of the Lord? Or who may stand in His holy place? He who has clean hands and a pure heart, Who has not lifted up his soul to an idol, Nor sworn deceitfully. He shall receive blessing from the Lord, And righteousness from the God of his salvation.

Psalm 97:10-12 (New Living Translation)You who love the Lord, hate evil! He protects the lives of his godly people and rescues them from the power of the wicked.

Proverbs 3:30 (New International Version) Do not accuse anyone for no reason—when they have done you no harm.

Proverbs 3:31-32 (New International Version) Don't envy violent people or copy their ways. Such wicked people are detestable to the Lord, but he offers his friendship to the godly.

Proverbs 9:6 (New Living Translation) Leave your simple ways behind, and begin to live; learn to use good judgment.

Proverbs 10:32 (New Living Translation) The lips of the godly speak helpful words, but the mouth of the wicked speaks perverse words.

Proverbs 15:3 (New Living Translation) The Lord is watching everywhere, keeping his eye on both the evil and the good.

Proverbs 16:13 (New Living Translation) The king is pleased with words from righteous lips; he loves those who speak honestly.

Proverbs 18:2 (New Living Translation) Fools have no interest in understanding; they only want to air their own opinions.

Proverbs 22:6 (New Living Translation) Direct your children onto the right path, and when they are older, they will not leave it.

Proverbs 27:23 (King James Version) Be diligent to know the state of your flocks, *And* attend to your herds.

Proverbs 29:11 (New Living Translation) Fools vent their anger, but the wise, quietly hold it back.

Ecclesiastes 4:4 (New Living Translation) Then I observed that most people are motivated to success because they envy their neighbors. But this, too, is meaningless—like chasing the wind.

Isaiah 30: 8-9 (New Living Translation) Now go and write down these words. Write them in a book. They will stand until the end of time as a witness that these people are stubborn rebels who refuse to pay attention to the LORD's instructions

Jeremiah 17:9 (New Living Translation) The human heart is the most deceitful of all things, and desperately wicked. Who really knows how bad it is?

Ezekiel 22:30-31 (New King James Version) So I sought for a man among them who would make a wall, and stand in the gap before Me on behalf of the land, that I should not destroy it; but I found no one. Therefore I have poured out My indignation on them; I have consumed them with the fire of My wrath; and I have recompensed their deeds on their own heads," says the Lord God.

Matthew 19:14-15 (New Living Translation) But Jesus said, "Let the children come to me. Don't stop them! For the Kingdom of Heaven belongs to those who are like these children." And He placed His hands on their heads and blessed them before He left.

Mark 7:32-35 (New Living Translation) A deaf man with a speech impediment was brought to him, and the people begged Jesus to lay his hands on the man to heal him. Jesus led him away from the crowd so they could be alone. He put his fingers into the man's ears. Then, spitting on his own fingers, he touched the man's tongue. Looking up to heaven, he sighed and said, "Ephphatha," which means, "Be opened!" Instantly the man could hear perfectly, and his tongue was freed so he could speak plainly!

Luke 1:26-28 (New Living Translation) In the sixth month of Elizabeth's pregnancy, God sent the angel Gabriel to Nazareth, a village in Galilee, to a virgin named Mary. She was engaged to be married to a man named Joseph, a descendant of King David. Gabriel appeared to her and said, "Greetings, favored woman! The Lord is with you!

John 5:8-9 (New Living Translation) Jesus told him, 'Stand up, pick up your mat, and walk!'

Romans 8:24-27 (New Living Translation) We were given this hope when we were saved. If we already have something, we don't need to hope for it. But if we look forward to something we don't yet have, we must wait patiently and confidently. And the Holy Spirit helps us in our weakness. For example, we don't know what God wants us to pray for. But the Holy Spirit prays for us with groanings that cannot be expressed in words.

2 Corinthians 5:18-19 (New Living Translation) All of this is a gift from God, who brought us back to himself through Christ. And God has given us this task of reconciling people to him. For God was in Christ, reconciling the world to himself, no longer counting people's sins against them. And he gave us this wonderful message of reconciliation.

Ephesians 4:23-27 (New Living Translation) Instead, let the Spirit renew your thoughts and attitudes. Put on your new nature, created to be like God—truly righteous and holy. So stop telling lies. Let us tell our neighbors the truth, for we are all parts of the same body. And "don't sin by letting anger control you." Don't let the sun go down while you are still angry, for anger gives a foothold to the devil.

1 Thessalonians 5:9-11 (New Living Translation) For God chose to save us through our Lord Jesus Christ, not to pour out his anger on us. Christ died for us so that, whether we are dead or alive when he returns, we can live with him forever. So encourage each other and build each other up, just as you are already doing.

James 5:16 (New International Version) Confess your sins to each other and pray for each other so that you may be healed.

Colossians 4:2 (New King James Version) Continue earnestly in prayer, being vigilant in it with thanksgiving;

Psalm 23:1-6 (adaptation) Yea, though we walk through the valley of the shadow of death, we will fear no evil; For You are with us; Your rod and Your staff, they comfort us. You prepare a table before us in the presence of our enemies; You anoint our heads with oil; Our cup runs over. Surely goodness and mercy shall follow us All the days of our lives; And we will dwell in the house of the Lord forever.

Psalms 94:17 (New Living Translation) Unless the Lord had been my help, my soul had almost dwelt in silence.

Proverbs 10:21 (King James Version) The lips of the righteous feed many: but fools die for lack of wisdom.

Proverbs 16:13 (King James Version) Righteous lips are the delight of kings; and they love him that speaketh right.

Proverbs 18:10 (English Standard Version) The name of the Lord is a strong tower; the righteous runneth into it and is safe.

Isaiah 5:18 (New Living Translation) What sorrow for those who drag their sins behind them with ropes made of lies, who drag wickedness behind them like a cart!

Isaiah 60:22 (New Living Translation) A little one shall become a thousand, and a small one a strong nation. I, the Lord, will hasten it in its time.

Corinthians 1:3-5 (New Living Translation) All praise to God, the Father of our Lord Jesus Christ. God is our merciful Father and the source of all comfort. He comforts us in all our troubles so that we can comfort others. When they are troubled, we will be able to give them the same comfort God has given us. For the more we suffer for Christ, the more God will shower us with his comfort through Christ. Even when we are weighed down with troubles, it is for your comfort and salvation! For when we ourselves are comforted, we will certainly comfort you. Then you can patiently endure the same things we suffer. We are confident that as you share in our sufferings, you will also share in the comfort God gives us.

I Peter 3:12 (King James Version) For the eyes of the LORD are on the righteous, And His ears are open to their prayers; But the face of the LORD is against those who do evil.

I John 4:7-8 (New Living Translation) Dear friends, let us continue to love one another, for love comes from God. Anyone who loves is a child of God and knows God. But anyone who does not love does not know God, for God is love.

Isaiah 65:23-24 (King James Version) They shall not labor in vain, nor bring forth for trouble; for they are the seed of the blessed of the Lord, and their offspring with them. And it shall come to pass, that before they call, I will answer; and while they are yet speaking, I will hear.

1 Samuel 14:7 (New King James Version) So his armor bearer said to him, "Do all that is in your heart. Go then; here I am with you, according to your heart.

James 5:13-18 (New King James Version) Is anyone among you suffering? Let him pray. Is anyone cheerful? Let him sing psalms. Is anyone among you sick? Let him call for the elders of the church, and let them pray over him, anointing him with oil in the name of the Lord. And the prayer of faith will save the sick, and the Lord will raise him up. And if he has committed sins, he will be forgiven. Confess your trespasses to one another, and pray for one another, that you may be healed. The effective, fervent prayer of a righteous man avails much. Elijah was a man with a nature like ours, and he prayed earnestly that it would not rain; and it did not rain on the land for three years and six months. And he prayed again, and the heaven gave rain, and the earth produced its fruit.